"I applaud the brilliant work of Bob Klitgaard's *Prevail*. . . . Its messages are presented with a unique kind of engaging erudition that has much to offer for general audiences as well as more academic ones. Buy, read, share *Prevail* with friends, family, and colleagues."

—PHILIP ZIMBARDO
President & Founder, Heroic Imagination Project

"Whether you are seeking solutions to dilemmas that you are confronting or deeper and better ways to think about them, Robert Klitgaard's wide-ranging book will give you lots to contemplate."

—HOWARD GARDNER
Harvard Graduate School of Education

"Robert Klitgaard is one of those rare professors who harnesses rigorous academic inquiry to big human questions, making his writing both insightful and relevant. With each new work, Klitgaard further journeys far beyond the status of academic intellectual to the role of wise teacher from whom we can all learn."

—JIM COLLINS
Author of *Good to Great*

"Reading Klitgaard's exploration of intimate partnerships will deepen your romantic love and result in a sustained experience of joy, passion, and human flourishing."

—KIMBERLY J. MILLER
Author of *Boundaries for Your Soul*

"Too often, life is about getting by, avoiding hardship and upheaval. That is a missed opportunity. In *Prevail*, Robert Klitgaard masterfully lays out the hero's path to ordinary greatness by seeing all of life as a calling. We all need this book."

—ARTHUR C. BROOKS
Harvard University

"*Prevail* gives us practical advice on how to face life's big challenges, based on the examples set by people who have lived lives that are full, not necessarily with accomplishments, but with service, gratitude, and intimacy."

—FRANCIS FUKUYAMA
Stanford University

"Presented very much from a Christian perspective, this excellent book actually reflects the wisdom of all the world's great religions. It provides invaluable resources and wonderful inspiration."

—DAVID ROSEN
International Director of Interreligious Affairs, American Jewish Committee

"After reading this book, I feel delighted and enriched. For all of us who face pivotal, or even cyclical, transitions and crises in our lives, this book provides guidance and wisdom. It does so with a playful lightness of touch that refreshes rather than weighs you down—indeed, a rare achievement. Drawing from a lifetime of reading broadly and working respectfully with peoples around the world, Klitgaard's synthesis is a blessing to us all."

—RONALD HEIFETZ
Harvard Kennedy School

"Bob Klitgaard, always a provocative thinker and teacher, has ventured into fascinating territory in this book. . . . *Prevail* offers glimpses of Klitgaard's global adventures and his own wisdom, perhaps best summarized in the recurring phrase 'both/and.' But it offers above all an extraordinary exploration of deep personal challenges and insights that draw on an unparalleled array of perspectives and wisdom."

—KATHERINE MARSHALL
Executive Director, World Faiths Development Dialogue

"This is an extraordinary book. . . . Drawing on his own deep learning and academic expertise and the personal insights of a lifetime, Bob Klitgaard sets out a brilliant framework of wisdom, experience, and understanding to help us on our way by discovering and developing heroism in our own lives and in the lives of others."

—JESSE NORMAN
Member of Parliament, United Kingdom

"If anyone can write a book that guides us in the midst of disruptions to make discerning decisions, Bob has something to say. As I face challenges big and small, I look forward to the nuggets of ideas and frameworks he provides to be some of my decision-making guideposts. I have made it a point not to read many books on the how-tos of leadership, so for this very reason *Prevail* is being read!"

—BARRY H. COREY
President, Biola University

Prevail

Prevail

How to Face Upheavals and Make Big Choices
with the Help of Heroes

ROBERT KLITGAARD

WIPF & STOCK · Eugene, Oregon

PREVAIL
How to Face Upheavals and Make Big Choices with the Help of Heroes

Wipf & Stock
An Imprint of Wipf and Stock Publishers
199 W. 8th Ave., Suite 3
Eugene, OR 97401

www.wipfandstock.com

PAPERBACK ISBN: 978-1-6667-9103-7
HARDCOVER ISBN: 978-1-6667-9102-0
EBOOK ISBN: 978-1-6667-9104-4

12/06/21

For Genevéve, Tamryn, Kai, and Kristen

On an aspirational account of self-creation, the creator does not determine, choose, or shape the created self; rather, she looks up to, imitates, and seeks to become the created self.

—AGNES CALLARD, *ASPIRATION*

Contents

Introduction

First, a quick word from our sponsor. Then we'll open it up for questions. (Admittedly, from me.)

A QUICK TAKE

"Robert Klitgaard advises governments and organizations around the world on how to face upheavals and make transformative decisions. Here he turns his attention to our 'big choices.' Moving across history, literature, philosophy, psychology, and everyday life, he shows how heroes can help us make transformative decisions about careers, romance, family, emigration, joining or leaving a religion or a political movement, and more. We see how to experiment with different callings, how to find and use big insights, and how to share and serve with compassion.

"We all confront upheavals and big choices, especially in these times of pandemics, economic turmoil, and dehumanization. We seek ideas and inspiration, not formulas or condescension. *Prevail* is erudite and engaging, full of twists and surprises and fascinating characters. In a world of skim-milk self-help, this is a book to savor and come back to, again and again."

Q AND A

So, what do you mean by "prevail"? What are we prevailing over?

We prevail over upheavals in our lives. We prevail by facing and making transformative choices about our lives. Think of the opposites: to bail and to flail. *Bailing* means avoiding big choices and responding to upheavals by dropping out. *Flailing* means slashing away at the whole idea of choices—if the world's upheavals show it's crazy, well, let's get just as crazy.

The prototype of bailing is a hermit. The extreme of flailing is an addict. Both end up alone in a kind of living death, meaning they are far away from a full human life of purpose, meaning, and people.

This book examines the prototype of *prevailing*: the hero in myth and legend, in literature and history, in religion and science, and all around us in everyday life. And even though we may think of ourselves as anything but heroic—we may think that's a cruel joke, applied to us—we can better face our own upheavals and guide our own big choices with the help of heroes.

How does that work? What kind of help can Ulysses or Harry Potter or Martin Luther King Jr. give me?

Like you, heroes face crises. They must make decisions about whom to become. In doing so, they discover or receive a calling, meaning a deep sense of purpose in and for their life choices. They also find or are given a big "aha!," meaning a deep insight that makes sense of contradictions in themselves and also in the world around them. They feel gratitude, as if the calling and insight were not their achievements but gifts that they didn't in some sense deserve. And then they go out into the crazy, imperfect world to share their calling and insight and to serve others with compassion.

I'm not saying you must have a "hero," but rather that heroic examples can inspire us. And as we make big, confusing choices those steps of calling, insight, gratitude, and serving can guide us.

That sounds noble. Does it work?

"It" is a schema—a kind of hero's path—a framework for us to play with as we try to make sense of our upheavals and big choices. For example, the book shows how we can probe the idea of a calling in our lives. Some lucky people don't even have to ask—they know from early on whom they should become. In the book we see examples of stained-glass-window makers, philosophers, conductors, and Buddhist monks. Most of us don't know our calling, and the book suggests we shouldn't try to figure it out as if we were manipulating a spreadsheet. Rather, we should *experiment* with ourselves. In the book, we look at five big categories of callings with some inspiring examples, and then we consider how we might try out one or more of them.

The same goes for those big ahas that suddenly enlighten us about ourselves and the world. One chapter uses four big insights to lay out a general pattern: what they do, how they are learned and passed along, and how they can slide from useful insight into pernicious ideology. And this morphology of insights, if you will, leads to suggestions about how we might acquire and manage them.

I imagine big insights can do bad things as well as good things. They can lead to intolerance. Many evil things in the world have resulted from dogmatic callings and insights.

True. A calling can be in some sense malevolent, and a big insight can be arresting but invalid. We can't afford to be gullible or cavalier. We have to scrutinize sudden feelings of purpose and sudden gleams of seeming understanding. One way is to experiment with them for a time and see what happens. Another way involves heroes again. If you feel a calling, find exemplars who share it and learn from them. If your brain shivers from a big insight, find the best of those who have had the insight and evaluate their trajectories.

The absence of a calling and insight in our lives means that upheavals can blow us away, that temptations can overwhelm us. If we are rudderless and ignorant, we may readily give up and bail. Or we may declare that the world is meaningless and decide just to grab whatever we can—in other words, we flail.

In the book you talk about "transformative choices." What are they?

These are decisions that involve two things: deep uncertainty and deciding for our future selves. Transformative choices include what to study or what career to embark upon. Embracing a particular religion or leaving it. Moving across the country or around the world. Whether to get married. If and when to have children. Transformative choices force us to imagine ourselves in the future—what we will approve of then, what we will abhor—which of course we can't now know. At the same time, what we choose will shape our future selves. We're trying to decide in some sense for someone we don't know and can't know, about uncertain consequences set in a future that could be qualitatively different.

This is the opposite of cranking out the costs and benefits of purchasing a car or vacationing in Canada. It is existential. As a result, transformative decisions themselves can create upheavals for us. They too can kindle the responses of bailing and flailing.

Enter here the hero and those stages of calling, insight, gratitude, and sharing and serving. Heroes can inspire us as we face transformative decisions. They help us make sense of our confusion. They elevate our hearts and minds. Their examples motivate us, not to copy them in detail, because their situations are not ours, but by illustrating ways to cope, how to have courage, and options and behaviors that might not have occurred to us. They help us imagine the best future selves we might be—and how our choices can make those selves more likely.

And that heroic path can remind us to revisit our own callings, insights, and possible ways to share and serve in the future. To paraphrase the philosopher Agnes Callard, the person making a transformative choice should look up to, imitate, and seek to become the created self; and I think our particular heroes and the framework of the heroic path can help us envision that created self.

Can heroes also help us with our quite unheroic everyday lives?

A saint once said that just as God's love is present in the little things of life, so too should our love be. Heroes inspire us not just through great deeds but also through their way of being, which we try to translate to our everyday lives. One chapter in the book deals with romance and intimacy. Falling in love can be deepened by the couple's developing a joint calling, sharing big insights, and then serving others together.

Not to be a downer here, but families sometimes break up, and marriages all too often end in divorce. More to the point of your book, heroes fail. The saints and sinners of one era can have their signs reversed in another. What does this mean for your model?

Chapter 1 begins with short case studies of breakdowns in one's calling, worldview, and chosen way of sharing and serving. Chapter 6 describes how insights can erode into ideologies. In Chapter 10 we confront backsliding—where we know what we want to do and should do, but then don't do it. These chapters, and I hope the whole book, can help us do better despite our failures and shortcomings.

But to your bigger point about the imperfections of heroes: even for the devout, perfect enlightenment is only for the holy few, and God became man only once. A big insight of both Buddhism and Christianity concerns the radical imperfection and incompleteness of human beings. This is an insight of all religions, really; and yet all religions also depict the lives we should aspire to live, through their teachings and also through the examples of their founders and the many heroes of faith who have followed them.

Speaking of religion: from the beginning of your book, when you relay the teachings of Thomas à Kempis, to the end, where you ask us to imagine ideal heroes, you evoke Christian themes. Is your book also for people who aren't Christians, or who may profess no religion at all?

A quick clarification before I answer your question. In the book the advice of Thomas à Kempis serves as a foil. His way of imitating Christ, I suggest, should not be ours. Chapter 6 depicts "the Protestant insight" with sympathy but also with a critique of its propensity to slide into a proud and judgmental ideology. Several chapters tell the stories of people who have lost their Christian faith. You won't find apologetics here—no proselytizing, no proclamations.

True, I hope that groups in churches and classrooms will find this book a catalyst for talking about Christian callings and insights, how to share and serve with love, topics like romance and intimacy, and backsliding. But the intended audiences are broader. People of other religions, or none, will feel welcome in these pages. Counselors, therapists, and human resource specialists will identify with the challenges here—and I hope they will glean practical ideas for themselves and the people they serve. Scholars are studying heroes through the varied lenses of the classics, literature, religion, history, sociology, psychology, and business. Few have braved their way across the disciplines and into practical recommendations, as this book, in all modesty and with trepidation, tries to do. Professors and students from these fields may enjoy finding here variations on some of their favorite themes—and ways to explore their own lives as well. (Appendix 1 provides discussion questions for each chapter.)

Most of all, this book is dedicated to people who are experiencing distress and facing life-defining choices. The world seems sick, and we may worry about contagion. We may feel overwhelmed, numb, and lost.

Assaulted by upheavals both social and personal, some of us may be tempted to *bail*—to withdraw from the insanity and simply decide no longer to play the game or run the race. Others of us may *flail*—demolishing the restraints of religion and family and society and being just as nuts as the world is.

Instead, this book proposes that we welcome into our lives the heroes of myth and legend, literature and history, religion and science, and everyday life. Their diverse callings, insights, and acts of compassion can encourage us and heal us. The heroic path can guide our own journeys from turmoil to transformation.

Heroes can help us *prevail.*

A Summary Flowchart

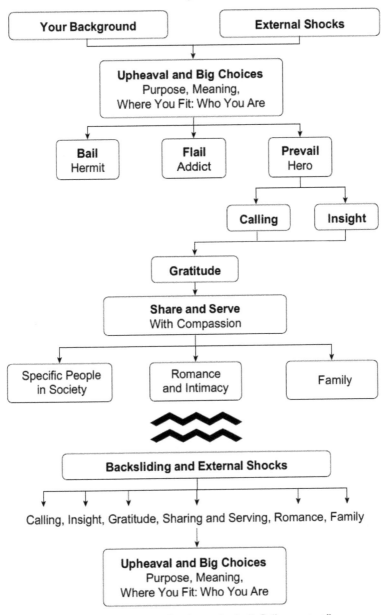

PART I

Bail, Flail, or Prevail

1

Upheavals and Big Decisions

This book is aimed at people who are experiencing upheavals and confronting transformative choices about careers, romance, family, emigration, joining or leaving a religion or a political movement, and more. Big disruptions and big decisions force us out of our comfort zones. They make us ask uncomfortable questions we haven't thought about for a long time, or ever. "What purpose do I have? What meaning do my choices contain? How should I, how could I, make a positive difference in the lives of others, including my loved ones?"

In the most extreme versions of upheaval and transition, a kind of existential crisis occurs. The world suddenly seems different from what we thought it was. Our feelings are numbed. "Is it worth it? Am I worth it? Whom should I become?"

EXAMPLES OF UPHEAVALS

Let's begin by considering some examples of personal upheaval.

Upheaval in Your Calling

Suppose you have joined a promising-sounding political movement or intellectual school of thought. Its purposes resonate with you, and you engage deeply. You draw part of your identity from the cause.

But, slowly or suddenly, you realize that they don't mean what they say, that the calling they proclaim is riddled with contradictions.

Consider this pinned tweet by Kat, a twenty-something woman from the United Kingdom:

> I initially joined the "woke movement" due to a feeling of solidarity with other marginalized groups. What I realized was, it's not about:
>
> - Solidarity: it creates division amongst people based on certain "identities," even between different minorities.
> - Equality: it creates hierarchies based on certain "identities."
> - Improvements: it wants to dismantle.
> - Inclusivity: it excludes people from the "wrong identities."
> - Compassion: it's about hatred, revenge, and anger.
> - Diversity: it wants everyone to think and behave the same way.
> - Lessening discrimination and stigma: it creates more.
> - Liberation: it thrives on authority and control.
>
> My understanding of the world was shattered.[1]

Note that word "shattered." If you experience the upheaval of disillusionment, you may feel broken, swing erratically between sadness and anger, and lose your calling.

Upheaval in Your Big Insight

Aella is the pseudonym for an American blogger in her late twenties. She was home-schooled in a stridently Christian family. She calls her father a stay-at-home, professional proselytizer. She ardently absorbed his Christianity. She recalls praying on her knees with tears of joy. As a teen, Aella won awards for her mastery of Scripture. She enjoyed apologetics: like a fencer, she could parry any argument against the fortress of fundamentalist doctrine.

And then, in her first year of college, an intellectual argument blasted a hole in her cognitive armature. "The argument jolted me so badly that I saw my own worldview from the outside, and it was all suddenly apparent to me how much patchwork I had needed for my defense, how teetering it was, all of the rationalizations I had pulled and twisted every which way. I was living

---

1. Tweet by @Ka_tastrophy, December 14, 2020.

in a structure built for defense, to which function came secondary . . . Did it function? Yes, but I'd never before seen how *ugly* it was."

Aella compared the new argument to a loud noise that precipitates an avalanche. An echo in the mountains does nothing unless a buildup of snow is ready to fall.

> Sitting there in that dorm room, I could feel my faith slipping away from my fingertips, and it was like trying to avoid a car crash in slow motion. No, no no no. I scrambled for answers, but all the ones I had studied so well suddenly seemed far away. I cried out to God to save me, because I couldn't do it myself. It was a desperate, last plea to my beautiful savior and friend, and the silence I got back was utter despair.
>
> The life I had known died right there. The way I knew the world—my education, my society, my purpose, my understanding of ethical behavior, of sex, obedience, submission, logic, origin of the universe—all of it crumbled around me and I suddenly knew nothing.[2]

Upheaval in Your Sharing and Serving

Suppose you've been working in a field where you proudly served others with compassion. But slowly or suddenly, you've come to feel numb to that calling. Your service seems to you ineffective, even pointless, and you begin to feel bitter that the people you help aren't grateful.

In a pioneering paper on burnout, the psychologist Christina Maslach asked: "What happens to people who work intensely with others, learning about their psychological, social or physical problems? Ideally, the helpers retain objectivity and distance from the situation without losing their concern for the person they are working with. Instead, our research indicates, they are often unable to cope with this continual emotional stress and burnout occurs. They lose all concern, all emotional feeling, for the persons they work with and come to treat them in detached or even dehumanized ways."[3]

Josh Cohen, who is both a psychoanalyst and a professor of literary theory, is the author of the 2019 book *Not Working: Why We Have to Stop.* He extends the concept of burnout beyond the helping professions, indeed beyond the workplace. "Burnout has something to do with a feeling of fundamental inadequacy in the face of the tasks life imposes on us. Not

---

2. Aella, "Lost My Faith." Used with her permission.
3. Maslach, "Burned-Out," 16.

just work tasks, but the tasks of relationships, of personal administration, everything really—everything that it takes to live and survive in the world."

Burnout is a malaise of inadequacy; it contains a sense of failure. "That's also part of what makes the difference between simple exhaustion—which we all feel—and burnout. Burnout has something to do with being overburdened by a set of self-imposed (or externally imposed, but heavily internalized) expectations."[4]

Some people have compared burnout to a dead battery. Maslach has a different analogy: "Like a wire that has just too much electricity, the worker emotionally disconnects."[5] If you suffer burnout, you may wonder if you should just let it all go.

TRANSFORMATIVE DECISIONS

Not all upheavals are negative. Suppose you have fallen in love: you may feel both enthralled and confused about your future. If you experience a financial windfall, you may celebrate and then, with a smile, realize you're at a loss about what this means for the way you will live your life.

Suppose you are a talented young person who faces big choices about your next steps—after graduation, say. People keep asking you, "So now, what are you going to do? Who are you going to become?" (Similar questions arise for older people, too, especially during employment transitions. Projecting from current data, the average American worker will change jobs ten times over a forty-year career.)

So many possibilities. Having to choose carries the opportunity cost of leaving options behind. "People actively avoid spending time thinking about big decisions," note Samuel Zimmerman and Tomer Ullman. "Transformative decisions may be difficult insofar as they force us to let go of that part of ourselves. *Torschlusspanik* ["gate shut panic"] is painful in and of itself, but it may particularly be painful when we are the ones shutting the gate."[6]

Perhaps you hadn't really focused on life after graduation. When you do, you may suddenly realize that what other people deem a flourishing life, phrased in occupational or familial terms, strikes you as insufficient, even banal. You may feel lost, questioning yourself and the world.[7]

4. Cohen, "Best Books on Burnout."

5. Maslach, "Burned-Out," 16.

6. Zimmerman and Ullman, "Models of Transformative Decision-Making," 96–97.

7. Søren Kierkegaard elaborates: "Possibility then appears to the self even greater and greater, more and more things become possible, because nothing becomes actual. At last it is as if everything were possible—but this is precisely when the abyss has

BAIL, FLAIL, OR PREVAIL

When you're faced with upheavals or have to make transformative decisions, it is good to seek out role models in your domain—work, parenting, sports . . . Listen to them, share with them, and learn.

And then look bigger. The heroes of myth and literature, of history and religion, also can instruct and inspire you. What's more, their stories echo with the challenges and choices you face.

They too were buffeted by crises, both societal and personal.

They too faced the unknown outside themselves in a chaotic world, and the unknown inside themselves as well.

And their life trajectories can inspire you. In all their diversity, there's often a pattern to their journeys.

- They found or received a *calling*—an emotional assurance that a particular purpose was theirs.

- They discovered or were given a big *insight*—a cognitive aha! that suddenly made sense of contradictions in themselves and in the world.

- And then—guided by their calling, enlightened by their insight, motivated by gratitude—they entered into their crazy, sinful, unwelcoming worlds to *share and serve*. They did so with compassion, empathy, and love.

The idea is not that you should adopt one of them as your personal hero. Rather, their stories contain lessons for your own transformative choices, where you make decisions about trajectories in your life under conditions of deep uncertainty and where the very choices you make will change you. Should you study this or that (or none of the above), enter or leave this career, move across the country or around the world, embrace or reject this religion, go professional where you are now an amateur, get married, become a parent? Transformative choices are different from size-up-and-solve spreadsheets. When you make them, you are deciding whom to become. The steps on the hero's journey can help you find your bearings and move ahead boldly.

More intimately, the hero's path can help you with your love life. Those steps of calling, insight, and serving can deepen what Iris Murdoch called "a

---

swallowed up the self . . . At the instant something appears possible, and then a new possibility makes its appearance, at last this phantasmagoria moves so rapidly that it is as if everything were possible—and this is precisely the last moment, when the individual becomes for himself a mirage." Kierkegaard, *Sickness unto Death*, 29.

process of unselfing wherein the lover learns to see, and cherish and respect, what is not himself."[8]

But first you and I have to get by an understandable reaction to a world gone crazy. Pandemics unleashed. Racism unmasked. Droughts, fires, and floods. Wars and insurrections. Cruelty baked into our customs and institutions.

Forget it, we may say—let's leave behind colleges and so-called careers, forgo romance and having a family. Let's become hermits or monks. (But not together—you somewhere and me somewhere else, far, far away.)

8. Murdoch, *Metaphysics*, 16–17

2

Ascetics and Addicts

I'm finishing this book in monk mode in a cabin in semirural Bhutan. No, I haven't donned a habit or joined a monastery. But monk mode yes, in the sense of cloistering myself right now from the flux of life. Avoiding extraneous activities and people. Focusing on writing. After weeks and months on the same task, I hope creativity emerges. On my small scale, breakthroughs too.

But this is nothing like what real monks do, or why.[1] My motivation is to wall off the world to concentrate on a big task. Ascetic monks have deeper purposes. They undertake voluntary practices of self-discipline to achieve a higher state of being.

Over the centuries and across many faith traditions, the goals of "participating in the divine nature" and "escaping the corruption that is in the world"[2] have driven people to monastic life. Theravada Buddhism provides one example. Theravada monks do not get much involved in the world outside; their quest for enlightenment is for their own liberation, not humankind's. They are ascetics, meaning "practicing strict self-denial as a measure of personal and especially spiritual discipline" (*Merriam-Webster*). They cannot eat after midday or handle money. They refrain from acquiring, except what is freely given to them. They avoid intoxicants and sex. Silence is preferred to "wrong speech," such as lying, idle chatter, or gossip. Some of

1. A quick word about sometimes-gendered nouns. As "actor" has become a gender-neutral term, so I will eschew "nun," "heroine," and other such nouns. Throughout the book, "heroes" refer to women and men.

2. 2 Peter 1:4.

them flee the secular world completely, with such disciplines as living in the forest, living under a tree, living in the open air, living in a cemetery, and sleeping in a sitting position without ever lying down.[3]

An ascetic tradition has been found in many religions, as Arthur Schopenhauer noted long ago. He branded the ascetic's avoidance of the world a "denial of the will to life."[4] Consider a compelling and disorienting example: Thomas à Kempis's *The Imitation of Christ* (1441). It has been called the most widely read book in Christianity aside from the Bible.[5] Thomas created it as a series of teaching aides for young monks in the monastery where he resided almost six hundred years ago.

It's an exotic primer to an archetypal reaction to an evil, crazy world— just bail. One we should try to understand.

AVOID THE WORLD

Thomas tells his monks, and by extension us, to seek Christ in everything we do, and also not to do many things. He advises against too many friends and too much knowledge, against women in general, and against the pleasures of the world. He recommends instead solitude, quiet, and the negation of self. Monk mode, in the Theravada sense.[6]

But Thomas goes further. We should not just avoid the world; we must abhor it. "And this is the supreme wisdom," he says, "to despise the world, and draw daily nearer to the kingdom of heaven."[7]

Thomas employs the metaphor of death.

---

3. Wilson, "Buddhism and Asceticism."

4. "Thus it may be that the inner nature of holiness, self-renunciation, mortification of self-will, asceticism, is here [in Schopenhauer's book] for the first time expressed in the abstract and free from all myth, as *denial of the will to life* . . . Although the whole body is only the visible expression of the will to life, the motives pertaining to this will are no longer active; indeed, the dissolution of the body, the end of the individual and therewith the greatest obstacle to the natural will, is welcome and desired." Schopenhauer, *World as Will*, 241, 254.

5. Kempis, *Imitation of Christ*. On its being the most widely read, see "Imitation of Christ."

6. Please abide the exaggeration of ideal types. In Catholicism, not all monks are like those Thomas à Kempis advises. Monks come in many varieties, including many such as the Taizé community who engage fully with people outside their monasteries (Moorhouse, *Beyond All Reason*). Later I will contrast Mahayana Buddhist monks with (most of those) in the Theravada tradition.

7. Kempis, *Imitation of Christ*, 27–28.

Learn now to die to the world, that you may begin to live with Christ. Learn now to despise all earthly things, that you may go freely to Christ.[8]

[Christ speaking, through the author] My son, you must needs be ignorant of many things: so consider yourself as dead, and crucified to the whole world.[9]

Blessed is the man who for Your sake, Lord, bids farewell to every creature, and, forcibly overcoming his natural inclinations, crucifies the desires of the flesh by the very fervor of his spirit, in order that he may offer you pure prayer with a quiet conscience. Having excluded all worldly things from his heart and life, he will be worthy to take his place in the choir of Angels.[10]

[Christ speaking, through the author] And the more completely a man renounces worldly things, and the more perfectly he dies to self by the conquest of self, the sooner will grace be given . . .[11]

To many readers, including me, Thomas's prescriptions are not only sobering but, to say the least, unintuitive. What on earth frightens him so? Are there alternatives besides what Thomas advises and what Thomas fears?

Thomas is afraid of the temptations of the physical being, which stunt the growth of the spiritual being. He believes Satan threatens everywhere, even in monasteries; and at one point Thomas says that monks of many years' standing are particularly vulnerable. He fears sin, which is to him a vivid and expansive category. His lexicon may be off-putting to modern readers: "crucify the desires of the flesh," "Satan," even "sin." Let's attempt a contemporary rendition of what he feared.

Suppose our inclination is to embrace life, not to avoid it. We want to discover the wonders of the world and revel in them. Suppose further that we think many of life's high points are the products of pleasure, status, and power. (If this is not true of you, dear reader, please bear with me—you may find yourself more accurately described later.)[12] Suppose we therefore de-

8. Kempis, *Imitation of Christ*, 59.

9. Kempis, *Imitation of Christ*, 150.

10. Kempis, *Imitation of Christ*, 158–59.

11. Kempis, *Imitation of Christ*, 212.

12. Emil Brunner described a version of intoxication with the world. "The natural 'inclination' of our heart and will is to seek ourselves. Like the rapacious spider that sits in the center of his web, we sit in the midst of our world in a spirit of acquisitiveness. We want men and what men have, their happiness, their possessions, their honor, their power. All this is our booty. But we want also from men their love, their respect, their time, and their sympathy. Our Ego sits like a king enthroned and demands that the world serve it. My wife, my children, my school, and—yes, even my dear God, are all to

sign our lives to attain pleasure, status, and power. Many of the pleasures are a function of money, so we seek money. Status and power are influenced by factors that we can't help, such as class and gender and ethnicity and innate endowments, and also by things we can help at least in part, such as education, style, and career. So, we pursue money, and we choose our education, style, and jobs to enhance our status and power.

A stark and unflattering characterization. To appreciate Thomas à Kempis, let's go further.

Suppose the most extreme *pleasures* are thrilling activities, intoxication, sexual union, and what might be called personal magic. The last means the surge you feel when you solve a difficult problem, play a beautiful piece of music, make a splendid soufflé, win a big tennis match, or otherwise display your personal excellence.

Suppose the most extreme experiences of *status and power* are exclusive. People crave access to benefits others cannot partake. They seek the power to make decisions that others will or must follow.

What's the problem, then? Arguably, today's world contains more opportunities for pleasure than most people could enjoy at most times in history. Arguably, people have more opportunities for thrilling experiences, intoxication, sexual union, and personal magic than ever before. Arguably, the average person today has more access than ever before to important places and decisions that in the past were restricted to a privileged few. In many countries, "dignity has been democratized as political systems have progressively granted rights to wider and wider circles of individuals."[13] You may disagree with these assertions, but let's play with them for a moment and ask two questions.

If they were true, would people today experience greater levels of happiness and fulfillment and joy than in centuries past? Would people start to have enough of these pleasures and enough status and power so that they would seek something more?

I think the answer to both questions may be no, at least for many people. In this sense, Thomas à Kempis has a point. Imagine Thomas stating, "I do not believe that people are on average better off with greater access to alcohol and drugs than with less, with greater sexual freedom than with less, and with greater opportunities to display their personal magic, because

---

serve 'me.' *I* am the Lord my God. Some maintain the primacy of the ego with delicacy, others coarsely; but all maintain it. So is the natural man, the unconverted man, the godless, loveless man. If any believes that I have made too harsh a judgment let him speak for himself. I confess in any case that *I* am such a man—and those I know are such people." Brunner, *Our Faith*, 99–100.

13. Fukuyama, *Identity*, 91.

all these things lead people away from God." Thomas is also skeptical of the corruption of people who focus on status and power, and so he advocates the opposite: humility and obedience.

The extremes Thomas fears are:

- drug addicts so intoxicated with intoxication that they end up with bad health, confusion, and paradoxically the inability to experience real pleasure;

- sexually promiscuous people so dedicated to conquests and orgasms that sexual union becomes jaded and unsatisfying;

- people so obsessed with their personal magic that they become less interested in the magic for its own sake and more interested in how their magic compares with other people's—in which case, the magic can disappear;

- people so preoccupied with status and power that they become abusive and corrupt.

We can see why these cases would make Thomas cringe. And through them we can better appreciate his recommendation to withdraw from the world.

In these extreme cases, we perceive the opposite of Thomas's own recommended escape from life. But think about this similarity. The extreme drug addict also experiences a kind of living death (see Box 1). Not the living death of Thomas's ideal monk, holed away in self-denial and aspiring to a holy life that is not this one. But the extreme addict, who moves from dose to dose in a semiconscious stupor, with the highs less and less like those moments of joy the addict originally sought, may also end up alone in a cell, also far away from *a full human life*.

BOX 1. ADDICTION AND A LIVING DEATH

In the last chapter, we met Aella and experienced her personal upheaval with her faith. That wasn't the end of her travails. Two years later, when she was twenty-one, Aella became addicted to acid. For a period of forty weeks, she used 150–600 milligrams of acid every week. Unlike most acid users, who experience few or no symptoms of addiction, Aella felt hooked. She hated to lose the highs of insight and disorientation. "So I kept doing it. Again and again, in higher and higher doses."

And by the end of it, I barely got out of bed, barely ate. My sleep schedule became erratic, as I woke and slept as I wished. I had vivid lucid dreams. I had stopped working almost entirely and was living off slowly depleting savings. Why would I work? Why would I do anything? I was . . . not happy, not sad, I simply *was*. I was free of desire. I did not fear death.

And, ten months in, I realized that's what I was looking at—*death*. I would compulsively whisper "I am dead" under my breath throughout the day. I was an empty vessel. And I realized, that if I kept doing acid, I probably *would* die, out of sheer apathy.

So, Aella stopped using acid every week. Two years later, she wrote that she didn't really understand that decision, that "choosing life" seemed inevitable or "that it wasn't even a choice at all." Her journey back from living death to "normal" life took about ten months.[14]

THE OPPOSITE OF LIVING DEATH

A full human life? What does that mean?

Let's work toward it from the two versions of living death—from the side of the monk and from the side of the addict. Imagine the characterization in Figure 1.

A Full Human Life

Driven by Guilt   Driven by Anxiety

Ascetic   Addict

A Living Death

Figure 1

From a Living Death to a Full Human Life

14. Aella, "10 Months of Acid." Used with her permission.

Beginning at the lower left, the solitary ascetic, let us move upward to spiritual people trying to make their way and avoid sin. Consider one type, the kind Friedrich Nietzsche disparages when he has Zarathustra say, "Now I know what people sought formerly above all else when they sought teachers of virtue. Good sleep they sought for themselves, and poppy-head virtues to promote it."[15] A good night's sleep as the ultimate: by this he means a person whose objectives are to feel no guilt, to be materially secure, and to wall off a little world of peace and quiet. Nothing is wrong with these three feelings per se; Nietzsche criticizes making them the purpose of one's life. He deplores people for whom the avoidance of guilty feelings becomes the ultimate objective, for whom comfort becomes the blessed state, for whom calmness towers over all other states of the world. In making these desirable feelings ultimate aims, such people may seem to us as well as to Nietzsche to be missing something more important in a full human life. I leave this as a thought to return to in a moment.

Now let's turn to the other limiting case, the living death of the extreme addict. From the lower right, let us move up the figure to materialistic, pleasure- and status-seeking people who are not, however, self-destructive addicts. They are preoccupied with how well they are doing compared with others or with socially instigated styles. Their daily concerns are with things that even they, in moments of reflection, may admit are superficial signs of "success." These people are characterized by anxiety rather than guilt, by a concern for status rather than security. They make the avoidance of anxiety and the achievement of status the ultimate aims, and they often find that these are unattainable because there is always one more thing to buy, one more rung to climb, one more task left undone.

What is at the top of the circle? What ideal of a full human life that escapes both guilt and anxiety and represents the opposite of both kinds of living death?

15. Nietzsche, *Thus Spake Zarathustra*, 16.

3

Heroes

Across many cultures, one finds myths and examples of heroes. What "hero" means varies, and heroic lives are diverse. But what they have in common is a flourishing life that is the opposite of the living death of the extreme hermit or the hopeless addict. The hero is also far away from lives that concentrate on pleasure and status, or on security and peace. Heroes transcend selfish conceptions of the ultimate good. They accept the wonder of an individual calling and revere the possibility of a deeply felt and transforming insight. They address, indeed embrace, the imperfections of this world.

But what exactly are "heroes"? First we'll consider their dizzying variety, then an abstraction of how they go from upheaval through transformative decisions to prevailing—and to a full human life.

MANY KINDS OF HEROES

"The words 'epic' and 'hero' both defy generalization, let alone universalizing definitions," the classicist Gregory Nagy states in the first sentence of "The Epic Hero." The great medieval scholar Ernst Robert Curtius concluded, "A comparative phenomenology of heroism, heroic poetry, and the heroic ideal is yet to be given us."[1] And yet, patterns have been discerned.

For example, the Greek epic hero is characterized by three elements:

---

1. Curtius, *European Literature*, 170.

1. The hero is unseasonal.

2. The hero is extreme—positively (for example, "best" in whatever category) or negatively (the negative aspect can be a function of the hero's unseasonality).

3. The hero is antagonistic toward the god who seems to be most like the hero; antagonism does not rule out an element of attraction—often a "fatal attraction"—which is played out in a variety of ways.[2]

"Unseasonal" means outside the usual pattern of life. Heroes leave the usual path or cycle. And this being out of season prods them, indeed enables them, to be heroic.[3]

We can compare ideas about heroes in other eras and through the eyes of many disciplines (see Box 2).

BOX 2. FIVE TAKES ON HEROES

The Hero in the Mishnah

Gibor, the Hebrew word for hero or mighty one, comes from the root *gavar*, which means to increase and overflow, and it is also used to mean to overcome (adversaries and adversity). The sages of the Mishnah (last century before and first two centuries of the Common Era) had two well-known comments in response to their rhetorical question "Who is a hero?" One answer is "he who overcomes his passions (who exercises self-control)." The other is "he who turns his enemy into a friend."[4]

---

2. Nagy, *Ancient Greek Hero*, 1§50.

3. "The goddess of *being on time* [Hērā] makes sure that the hero [Hēraklēs or Hercules] should start off his lifespan by *being not on time* and that he should go through life by trying to catch up—and never quite managing to do so until the very end . . . And yet, without this unseasonality, without the disequilibrium brought about by the persecution of Hērā, Hēraklēs would never have achieved the equilibrium of immortality and the kleos or 'glory' that makes his achievements live forever in song." Nagy, *Ancient Greek Hero*, 1§45, 1§49.

4. Rabbi David Rosen, International Director of Interreligious Affairs, American Jewish Committee, personal communication, August 23, 2021.

The Hero in Europe in the Late Middle Ages

"The hero is the ideal personal type whose being is centered upon nobility and its realization—hence upon 'pure' not technical, values—and whose basic virtue is natural nobility in body and soul. The hero is distinguished by a superabundance of intellectual will and by its concentration against the instincts. It is this which characterizes his greatness of character. The specific virtue of the hero is self-control. But the hero's will does not rest here, it presses into power, responsibility, daring."[5]

The Shakespearean Hero

"The hero, with Shakespeare, is a person of high degree of public importance," writes A. C. Bradley, "and that his actions or sufferings are of an unusual kind. But this is not all. His nature also is exceptional." Bradley notes a classic feature of the Shakespearean hero: "In the circumstances where we see the hero placed, his tragic trait, which is also his greatness, is fatal to him."[6]

The Hero of Nineteenth-Century Romanticism

"He has to be made of pure gold; he has to be kind and dedicated, to suffer a trial by ordeal—loneliness and all that—and he must, absolutely must, be a man of genius. There are two strong reasons why the young rebel must be so outstanding. First, his excellence resolves the conflict between the conservatism and the progressivism within the romantic philosophy: the rebel is a progressive force, but he must be idolized, in order that there will be no widespread attempt to emulate him: the greatest majority are followers, and only a few can be leaders. Second, only the most excellent can transcend the tradition, yet thereby enrich it rather than destroy it."[7]

The Historical Hero

The philosopher Sidney Hook studied heroes in literature, music, and painting; philosophy and science; religion; and history. To Hook, "the historical hero" is not just an eventful person but an event-making person, "whose

5. Curtius, *European Literature*, 168, 167.

6. Bradley, *Shakespearean Tragedy*, 20, 21.

7. Agassi, "Genius in Science," 151.

actions are the consequences of outstanding capacities of intelligence, will, and character rather than of accidents of position . . . [A] hero is great not merely in virtue of what he does but in virtue of what he is."[8]

===

"[T]he legendary heroes of mankind," wrote Carl Jung, "[are] the very ones who are looked up to, loved, and worshipped, the true sons of God whose names perish not . . . Their greatness has never lain in their abject submission to convention, but, on the contrary, in their deliverance from convention. They towered up like mountain peaks above the mass that still clung to its collective fears, its beliefs, laws, and systems, and boldly chose their own way."[9]

Less grandly, historian Paul Johnson's 2008 book *Heroes* provides amusing, elegant biographical portraits that eschew theory and even definitions and "approach heroism by example." Heroic behavior is found in all walks of life, he emphasizes. (One convincing chapter describes the excellent hostess as a heroic type.) The status of a particular hero can wane, and in a generation or less reverence can turn to scorn. In Johnson's distillation, heroes share four traits: independence of mind, commitment, ignoring public opinion, and courage.[10]

In a different vein, psychologists have studied how (predominantly American) respondents define heroes and their characteristics. One recent list of heroic attributes contained bravery, moral integrity, conviction, courageous, self-sacrifice, protecting, honesty, selfless, determined, saves others, inspiring, and helpful. Less common but frequently included: proactive, humble, strong, risk-taker, fearless, caring, powerful, compassionate, leadership skills, exceptional, intelligent, talented; and personable.[11]

The psychologists Scott Allison and George Goethals have a website with over 250 profiles of heroes.[12] They cluster these heroes in categories: activists, artists, celebrities, fictional, legendary, political, science, spiritual, sports, superheroes, unsung (45 of them), and war. In their 2013 book *Heroic Leadership*, they provide short biographical sketches of 100 heroes allotted to 10 alliterative categories: trending, transitory, transitional, tragic, transposed, transparent, traditional, transfigured, transforming, and transcendent. But when it comes to defining heroes, like Johnson, they

---

8. Hook, *Hero in History*, 99–100.

9. Jung, *Development of Personality*, §298.

10. Johnson, *Heroes*.

11. Kinsella et al., "Zeroing."

12. https://blog.richmond.edu/heroes/about/.

are reluctant: "we have argued that heroism is in the eye of the beholder, and that heroes are heroes to anyone who regards them as heroes."[13] In an earlier book, Allison and Goethals provide more guidance: "Whether they are rulers, parents, deities, or teachers, heroes are described as courageous, selfless, and skillful . . . they earn heroic status by handling these common challenges with uncommon courage and grace."[14]

"Simply put, then," writes the psychologist Philip Zimbardo, "the key to heroism is a concern for other people in need—a concern to defend a moral cause, knowing there is a personal risk, done without expectation of reward."[15]

Joseph Campbell, a literature professor, defined a hero as "someone who has found or achieved or has done something beyond the normal range of achievement. A hero properly is someone who has given his life to something bigger than himself, or other than himself."[16] Building on Jung's work, Campbell found a pattern in heroic lives. The hero leaves the everyday world and adventures into a dark place of supernatural wonder. He encounters fabulous forces and wins a decisive victory. He then returns, a changed person, and shares his bounty with others. Heroes depart from the ordinary in ways that involve or create a calling, experience some sort of initiation that imbues a realization about themselves and their place in the world, and return home.[17]

In this book, we play with an abstraction of the heroic path and apply it to everyday lives, including our own upheavals and big choices.

- Heroes experience a *calling*.

- They attain a big *insight* about themselves and the world.

- They feel *gratitude* for these gifts.

- And then they *share and serve* others, with compassion and love.

---

13. Allison and Goethals, *Heroic Leadership*, 4.

14. Allison and Goethals, *Heroes*, 28.

15. Zimbardo, "What Makes a Hero?"

16. Campbell, "Hero with a Thousand Faces" (interview).

17. "The two—the hero and his ultimate god, the seeker and the found—are thus understood as the outside and inside of a single, self-mirrored mystery, which is identical with the mystery of the manifest world. The great deed of the supreme hero is to come to the knowledge of this unity in multiplicity and then to make it known." Campbell, *Thousand Faces*, 31.

Figure 2

The Path to Prevailing

When I say "play with" this path, I mean that we will bracket interesting scientific questions about concepts and measures, causal modeling, and heterogeneity across cultures and eras, not to mention across individual lives. We will leave aside the possible genetic, cultural, and societal factors that influence the definition and emergence of heroes and their waxing and waning. We will not explore the gender dimensions of heroism.[18] We will forgo proofs ("Because of A, B, C, you must believe D") and disputation ("Others have said this and that, but really it's this other thing"). Instead, we will try to have some fun with concepts and examples of calling, insight, gratitude, and serving with compassion—and test them on ourselves.

CALLING

Whether religious or secular, a calling contains a sense of personal purpose: that *this* is what one is meant to do. A calling resides in the domain of feeling. It is subjective. In surveys, somewhere between a third and two-thirds of Americans report that a sense of calling is important in how they view their work.[19] A recent review of the psychological literature shows that perceiving a calling and creating opportunities to live out that calling are "associated with a plethora of positive career-related and well-being outcomes."[20]

To get the gist of a calling that is not necessarily religious, consider the psychologist Abraham H. Maslow's studies of "self-actualizing people," his term for the "more matured, more fully human" among us. Their basic needs of belongingness, affection, respect, and self-esteem are gratified. They are spontaneous, natural, "more easily themselves than other people."

18. Tatar, *Heroine with 1001 Faces*.

19. Dik and Duffy, *Job a Calling*, 17.

20. Dik et al., "Career Callings," 185.

What characterizes these people? "Self-actualizing people are, without one single exception, involved in something outside of themselves. They are devoted, working at something, something which is very precious to them—some calling or vocation in the old sense, the priestly sense. They are working at something which fate has called them to and which they work hard at and which they love, so that the work-joy dichotomy in them disappears."[21]

What does it mean to have a calling? "The best way to communicate these feelings to someone who doesn't intuitively, directly understand them is to use as a model 'falling in love.' This is clearly different from doing one's duty, or doing what is sensible and logical."[22]

The psychologists Jeanne Nakamura and Mihaly Csikszentmihalyi interviewed hundreds of successful painters, dancers, poets, novelists, physicists, biologists, and psychologists—all people who seemed to have crafted lives for themselves built around a consuming passion. Theirs were admirable lives, the sort that many people dream of having.

These people shared what the authors called "vital engagement." They had in common a "completeness of involvement or participation and marked by intensity. There is a strong felt connection between self and object; a writer is 'swept away' by a project, a scientist is 'mesmerized by the stars.' The relationship has subjective meaning; work is a 'calling.'"[23]

INSIGHT

Like a calling, an *insight* also creates an aha!, but now of a cognitive sort. It is objective in essence, not subjective as with a calling. A big insight provides meaning. It makes sense of many things that heretofore were mysterious or unconnected; it clarifies the world and oneself. The philosopher Bernard Lonergan concludes that an insight:

1. comes as the release to the tension of inquiry;

2. comes suddenly and unexpectedly;

3. is a function not of outer circumstances but of inner conditions;

4. pivots between the concrete and the abstract;

5. passes into "the habitual texture of one's mind."[24]

21. Maslow, *Farther Reaches*, 43
22. Maslow, *Farther Reaches*, 301.
23. Nakamura and Csikszentmihalyi, "Construction of Meaning," 86.
24. Lonergan, *Insight*, §1 Elements.

Like a calling, a big insight may seem simply to arrive. "Most new dis-coveries are suddenly-seen things that were always there," writes Suzanne Langer. "A new idea is a light that illuminates presences which simply had no form for us before the light fell on them. We turn the light on here, there, and everywhere, and the limits of thought recede before it."[25]

Often the calling or the insight, or sometimes both, originate with a "peak experience." Almost all Maslow's self-actualizing subjects had such experiences, which they described as "mystic" or "oceanic" or "a cognition of being." Their insights were "so profound as to remove neurotic symp-toms forever; or were followed by greater creativity, spontaneity, or expres-siveness; or produced a more or less permanently changed, more healthy world-view, and so on."[26] Recent social science studies "awe experiences," which "shift our attention away from ourselves, make us feel like we are part of something greater than ourselves, and make us more generous toward others."[27]

The hero of Herman Hesse's novel *The Glass Bead Game* describes his peak experiences as glimpses of reality.

> What gives these experiences their weight and persuasiveness is not their truth, their sublime origin, their divinity or anything of the sort, but their reality. They are tremendously real, some-what in the way a violent physical pain or a surprising natural event, a storm or an earthquake, seem to us charged with an entirely different sort of reality, presence, inexorability, from ordinary times and conditions . . . Later on we may start to ques-tion them or examine their significance, if that is our bent; but at the moment they admit no doubts and are brimful of reality. My "awakening" has a similar kind of intensified reality for me.[28]

SHARING AND SERVING

The hero feels *gratitude* for the calling and the insight, and then come *shar-ing and serving*. These are relational, in contrast to the individual's feeling (the calling) and thinking (the insight). In sharing and serving, the calling and the insight are not confined to the hero's own well-being or sanctifica-tion. They are dedicated to others.

25. Langer, *Philosophy in a New Key*, 8.
26. Maslow, *Psychology of Being*, 95.
27. Allen, *Science of Awe*, 2.
28. Hesse, *Glass Bead Game*, 395.

What does it mean to *share* a calling and an insight? It is usually not the same as teaching a scientific theory or demonstrating a chemical reaction. This kind of sharing is often artistic, through metaphor and myth, parable and philosophical abstraction; or the sharing can take place through a practical program of discipline and passion combined. One shares via actions, not words; by example, not decree.

Heroes *serve* the needy and the forgotten, even the sinners and the enemies of society. For heroism, writes Paul Johnson, "a different kind of quality is required, a moral power. It is this which, throughout the ages, has produced heroes, often in the most unexpected places."[29] The moral power? Service to others.

Sharing and serving, to be done well, must be attentive to situation, norms, and conventions. Sharing and serving should be tailored to the recipient—to a person's feelings, needs, fears, and level of preparation. As a hypothesis, I would suggest that effective sharing and serving presuppose a relationship. The relationship could be one of community, or it could be one of friendship or love.

Imagine you and I are lucky enough to receive sharing and service from another person. If that person is dour and impersonal—if we feel that they are simply doing a duty or, worse, a penance—we will not be happy even though we may be appreciative.[30] But if that person shares and serves with kindness, as if they want to share and serve for the delight it gives them, then we will receive it with joy.

Anne Colby and William Damon studied "moral exemplars" who served others in remarkable, sustained ways. These people exhibited "strong, enduring, and general *positivity* toward their lives, toward their work, and toward other people. What do we mean by 'positivity'? First, we are referring to an enjoyment of life, especially an enjoyment of the work they are doing—whether it is fighting for racial justice, helping the poor, or working for peace."[31]

The moral exemplar has a sense of humor, is humble, and can "see oneself as contributing to an ongoing effort, not a savior who is out to change the world."[32]

---

29. Johnson, *Heroes*, 8 of backmatter.

30. "We do not call *him* the best man, who is obliged unceasingly to resist his own impulses and is constantly at war with his own desires; we say this, rather, of the man whose inclinations are kindly and benevolent from the start, so that he simply does not fall into doubt and self-conflict." Schlick, "Meaning of Life," 125.

31. Colby and Damon, *Some Do Care*, 262.

32. Colby and Damon, *Some Do Care*, 272.

THE HERO'S EXAMPLE OF A FULL HUMAN LIFE

These reflections introduce an image of a full human life that we will explore in the chapters that follow.

Heroes seek, or are given, a calling. They are attentive to who they are or can be, nurturing this understanding through knowledge and experience, and they are open to answers that may appear rather than being deduced or derived.

Heroes gain, or are granted, a big insight that addresses a personal challenge as well as a social one. Heroes are fortunate, we might say; but they are also prepared and available for insight.

Heroes also feel fortunate. Their calling and big insight feels given to them, not earned. Heroes are characterized by gratitude and amazement.

And then they reach out to others. Heroes apprehend that sharing may best be through example and artistic expression, rather than through words. They also feel what might be called a non-verbal command to serve others with compassion and bravery.[33]

The full human life of the hero fills us with admiration. But heroes? And us? We're just ordinary people, trying to cope. How is all this relevant to non-heroes like you and me?

33. Max Weber observed: "It takes both passion and perspective. Certainly all historical experience confirms the truth—that man would not have attained the possible unless time and again he had reached out for the impossible. But to do that a man must be a leader, and not only a leader but a hero as well, in a very sober sense of the word. And even those who are neither leaders nor heroes must arm themselves with that steadfastness of heart which can brave even the crumbling of all hopes." Weber, *Politics as a Vocation*, 128.

4

For Non-Heroes Too?

A ll of that may be fine for heroes. But what does it for the rest of us, who are not heroes?

What's more, maybe we've picked up that we shouldn't try to be heroes. You may have heard this in the military: "A hero is a guy who gets the rest of us killed." Or in sports, as when a football coach tells his players, "Know your responsibility and stick with that. Don't try to be a hero."

In so-called tight cultures around the world, individuals are discouraged from standing out. "Who do you think you are?" Even in loose cultures one can find an aristocratic scorn for heroes. A friend warned Lord Wellington, "Beware of heroes—the more you come to know them, the less you will think of them."[1] Self-appointed heroes seem particularly dangerous; a cliché is "delusions of grandeur." "Nothing more exposes us to madness than distinguishing us [ourselves] from others, and nothing more contributes to maintaining our common sense than living in the universal way with multitudes of men."[2]

"I JUST WANT TO BE AVERAGE"

When he was fifteen years old, the last thing my brother Bill wanted was to be a hero. In fact, he earnestly desired to be a non-hero. He used to say, "I just want to be average." This desire did not go down well with the adults in his life.

1. Johnson, *Heroes*, 277.
2. Goethe, *Wilhelm Meister*, 59.

"But you're not average," a teacher or a coach or a parent would respond.

"I don't care!" Bill would answer sadly or angrily. "I just want to be average."

This is not unusual. Many of us flee the exceptional, perhaps in order to escape expectations—especially when the expectations are not our own. Anxiety can overwhelm us. So can guilt in cases where those expectations are not fulfilled. How much better it is to set our sights low. Asked why we flee, we may pose questions in return.

"Why should I study so hard?"

"Why should I train so hard?"

"Why should I try to be so good?"

When writing this chapter, I talked with Bill—now a great success as a person and as a professional. Did he recall his reaction in those days? He thought about it, and later that day he handed me a note with these recollections of what he felt then:

> Let go of those expectations—the ones you have of me, the ones you want me to have for myself. I'm not sure I can live up to them, I'm not sure I want what they bring. "A big fish in a small pond" lets me move more easily and find my own way. The confines of parental expectations conflict with self-discovery. Let the silt settle out of muddy water.
>
> At first it was liberating—an absence of nagging. In time another voice developed that set goals and objectives, blending the voice of my parents with my own perceptions and ability. There are interior truths that need to be discovered by direct experience. If I'm not average now, it's because of a confluence of innate ability with good fortune.
>
> There is a role for structure and obedience—but in my experience those became overblown with importance. There is also a role for emergence and discovery, but watch out for self-indulgence. Teachers are so much better when you're ready to learn. A clear mind finds things out and unintended things happen. That's happiness—a sudden realization of an unexpected truth.[3]

Bill became a CFO and CIO in a leading company in the world of clinical trials and digital medicine, a long-distance amateur cyclist, a philanthropist, and a wonderful husband and father. None of these was automatic. As Bill and every one of us finds out, it is not easy for us to study or train

---

3. Used with Bill's blessing.

or practice virtue. Even when we do, our "success" doesn't just depend on us. Achievements are often couched in relative terms. Where did you finish in the race? What was your class rank? Did you provide the most hours of service? Did you win the election? Even standardized tests are normed, meaning that your score depends on how well the others did who took the tests. Relative success introduces competition. Sometimes the people you compete with are unknown, but often they are colleagues and friends. Your being exceptional often means that someone you know and like won't be as exceptional. If you ask a young person who's fleeing from being exceptional why, and if you listen carefully, you may hear something about not wanting to look better than one's friends, not wanting to make others look bad. Or perhaps you'll hear, "I don't want to look worse than my friends. I don't want others to make me look bad."

"I WANT TO BE A HERO"

Interestingly, some of those who flee from words like "hero" have something in common with some of those who declare that being a hero is their goal. They may share low levels of achievement motivation.

The psychologist David McClelland and his colleagues studied what he called the need for achievement, or achievement motivation.[4] People with a low need for achievement tend also to be fearful of failure. In a psychological experiment, people were asked to play a special game of throwing rings over a peg. They were allowed to choose the distance. They could choose a lay-up toss right next to the peg, or a throw several feet away, or a heave from the other side of the room—or any distance in between.

People with high achievement motivation tended to choose distances where they had about a fifty-fifty chance of making the toss. People with low achievement motivation chose differently. They would select either a lay-up or a long-distance bomb. If they chose the lay-up, they would be virtually certain to make the shot. Failure would be rare. If they chose the across-the-room miracle shot, success would be rare; but since the shot was so difficult, no one could blame them for failure. Low achievement motivation, high fear of failure.

Some people with low achievement motivation say they want to be heroes. For example, McClelland found that if you ask high school students with low achievement motivation what they want to be when they grow up, they will tend to say one of two things. The first thing is that they don't want to be anything. The very different second thing is that they want to be

---

4. McClelland, *Achievement Motive*.

president of the United States, or discover a cure for cancer, or make a billion dollars. Failure can't be criticized, and isn't feared, because anyone can be a nothing, and only one in millions can be president.

David McClelland found that people could be trained to increase their achievement motivation. He showed this through experiments in the inner city, as well as with businesspeople, students, and people in India. The training involved several stages: self-recognition through a test, learning about various kinds of motivation and their effects, and practicing being achievement oriented.

In an almost forgotten book about economic development, McClelland showed that countries differed in average levels of need for achievement.[5] Later he argued that in cultures with low need for achievement a variety of treatments seemed able to raise that need for achievement, with ensuing increases in economic prosperity.

One of McClelland's examples of change involved Protestantism. He reviewed the old arguments of Max Weber that the capitalist revolution in Europe was associated with the Protestant revolution.[6] Causation is of course difficult to establish historically, but McClelland was sympathetic to Weber's thesis. McClelland cited newer evidence from Latin America. After people switched from Catholicism or atheism to evangelical Protestantism, they scored higher on his tests in need for achievement—and subsequently they had better family situations, lower levels of alcoholism and crime, and higher incomes.

McClelland's work carries three lessons. First, those who say they just want to be average and those who spout that they'd like to be heroes may have more in common than they realize. Second, simply saying that you want to be a hero isn't the same as achieving it—in fact, it may be a sign of low achievement motivation. Third, people can increase their achievement orientation. One way, at least for some people, is through formal training, and McClelland's techniques are today purveyed by private companies around the world.[7]

5. McClelland, *Achieving Society*.

6. Weber, *Protestant Ethic*.

7. A group called the Consortium for Research on Emotional Intelligence in Organizations provides a model program for training in achievement motivation at http://www.eiconsortium.org/model_programs/achievement_motivation_training.html.

TRAINING HEROES

The psychologist Philip Zimbardo supplements the hero of myth and romantic imagination with the hero of everyday life. He and several other psychological researchers on heroism argue that "it is possible to nurture a mind-set to help others in need, care for others compassionately, and to develop confidence in one's own ability to take heroic action."[8]

Zimbardo makes the useful distinction between heroic acts and heroic people. He and his colleagues estimate that about one-fifth of the U.S. population has carried out a heroic act.[9] His Heroic Imagination Project is designed to create everyday heroes, defined as those who act on behalf of others in need or in defense of a moral cause, aware of risks and personal costs.[10] And his bet is that conveying some "principles of social psychology" will lead to more heroic acts—a bet because, as he and others emphasize, more research is needed.

The principles come in three batches. First, trainees learn that "our mindsets—the set of beliefs we have about whether our abilities can be grown or changed—profoundly impact the way we work, play, explore, and live." In the context of improving the world, trainees learn why limiting beliefs occur and how to change them. Trainees learn that "their daily efforts to navigate challenges and failures and seek triumphs are valid and that doing these things can help make the world a better place."

Second, trainees learn that the opposite of a hero is not a villain but a *bystander*, someone who does nothing during adverse situations. Trainees learn "how to identify bystander behavior in various scenarios and what can be done to prevent it in oneself and in others."

Third, trainees learn about implicit and explicit biases. They learn how to identify their implicit biases and how to change them. The idea is apparently that prejudiced people are more likely to be bystanders.

Similar themes emerge in training by the Hero Construction Company, founded and led by the psychologist Matt Langdon.[11] In his program and Zimbardo's, a key audience is high school students. In both cases, some risks of hero training as well as possible benefits have been identified, but scientific evaluations of the outcomes and costs remain to be done. These are humble heroes—a theme to which we will return.

8. Franco et al., "Heroism Research," 5.

9. Zimbardo et al., "Exclusive and Inclusive," 221.

10. https://www.heroicimagination.org.

11. https://www.heroconstruction.org/who-we-are.

LEARNING FROM EXEMPLARS

Exemplars help us find our way to fuller human lives. We may be lucky enough to have different kinds, or levels, of exemplars.

1. A behavioral model teaches us specific skills needed for our positions within our chosen fields.

2. A role model exemplifies a specific calling such as a composer or a stained-glass maker. "Individuals use the role model attributes they observe as clues to creating their 'ideal self'—the self they would like to become. Role models are particularly helpful in imagining this ideal self because by observing role models, individuals can provisionally try out different styles or behaviors to see which ones best suit their developing style."[12]

3. A hero displays for us a full human life.

Ideally, our upbringing and education would expose us to all three: behavioral models, role models, and heroes. (We'll come back to these categories of exemplars later in the book.)

In their classic book *Corporate Cultures*, Terry Deal and Arthur Kennedy find that an organization's heroes reveal the organization's values.[13] Whom do employees cite when asked "Who are some people who have best represented the values of this company?" and "Who in the company do you most admire?" It is difficult for people to know what is meant when an organization urges them to be "good" or "productive"; it is easier to emulate specific exemplars. Importantly, the authors point out that when necessary corporate heroes go against the existing order to advance those values. Other fields, too, have emphasized learning from exemplars, "bright spots," and outliers.[14]

We can find exemplars and heroes in the real world. We can also seek them and learn from them in legend and literature.

In W. Somerset Maugham's novel *The Razor's Edge*, Larry Darrell is an exemplar of a full human life. As a young pilot in World War I, Larry loses his close friend, a particularly shattering experience because the friend was coming to his rescue. Larry launches into a search for meaning. He visits Europe, studies philosophy, and explores the artistic life. He works in a coal mine, where he discovers almost by chance that one of his fellow miners

12. Gibson, "Role Models," 702–3.

13. Deal and Kennedy, *Corporate Cultures*, ch. 3.

14. For example, Bronk, "Exemplar Methodology"; Heath and Heath, *Switch*, ch. 1; and Gladwell, *Outliers*.

happens to be a former priest who says he is fleeing God. The priest tells Larry about India, about a special guru in a mountain ashram.

Larry goes there. He meets a hero, the saintly Shri Ganesha. Larry is fascinated. He eventually dwells in a cabin on a Himalayan peak, where one dawn he is overwhelmed by a peak experience. He relates this experience later:

> "I was ravished with the beauty of the world. I'd never known such exaltation and such a transcendent joy. I had a strange sensation, a tingling that arose in my feet and travelled up to my head, and I felt as though I were suddenly released from my body and as pure spirit partook of a loveliness I had never conceived. I had a sense that a knowledge more than human possessed me, so that everything that had been confused was clear and everything that had perplexed me was explained. I was so happy that it was pain and I struggled to release myself from it, for I felt that if it lasted a moment longer I should die; and yet it was such rapture that I was ready to die rather than forego it. How can I tell you what I felt? No words can tell the ecstasy of my bliss. When I came to myself I was exhausted and trembling."[15]

Larry rejects the life of the solitary ascetic:

> "I felt in myself an energy that cried out to be expended. It was not for me to leave the world and retire to a cloister, but to live in the world and love the objects of the world, not indeed for them-selves, but for the Infinite that is in them . . . in those moments of ecstasy I had indeed been one with the Absolute . . . I was willing to accept every sort of life, no matter what its pain and sorrow; I felt that only life after life, life after life could satisfy my eagerness, my vigor and my curiosity."[16]

And so, having lived through his calling to find wisdom and having received an insight deep in his heart, the young man returns home to con-front the Depression, his former fiancée (now married), and a former friend who has been crushed by tragedy. Then Larry Darrell dedicates himself to sharing and serving.

No one recognizes Larry as a guru or a hero. No one, that is, except the novelist and the admiring readers of *The Razor's Edge*.

---

15. Maugham, *Razor's Edge*, 220.
16. Maugham, *Razor's Edge*, 222.

WHICH HERO?

If we have experienced a sense of rightness in a hero's saga, he or she may become our own source of strength. We may have faith in the power of that example to transform our lives and through us, we hope, the lives of others. With their stories close to our hearts, we can become more heroic—even if we are in no grand sense "heroes"—in our mundane lives.

An artistic analogy is useful. Our appreciation of beauty may in some sense hinge upon those especially gifted and experienced to create it. "The spirit of an artist's gifts can wake our own," notes Lewis Hyde. "We may not have the power to profess our gifts as the artist does, and yet we come to recognize, and in a sense to receive, the endowments of our being through the agency of his creation."[17]

In the same way, people vary in their abilities to find a calling, discover an insight, and live both calling and insight through sharing and serving. In our diversity, those of us who have less ability and experience may well find inspiration and instruction from those with more. "It is very similar in the domain of the religious consciousness, religious production, and revelation," Rudolph Otto wrote. "Here, too, most men have only the 'predisposition,' in the sense of a receptiveness and susceptibility to religion and a capacity for freely recognizing and judging religious truth at first hand . . . The prophet [or we might say, the hero] corresponds in the religious sphere to the creative artist in that of art: he is the man in whom the Spirit shows itself alike as the power to hear 'the voice within' and the power of divination, and in each case appears as a creative force."[18]

One question is how to identify heroes whose sagas are meaningful *for us*. Ideally, we would have heroes whose callings inspire us, whose insights speak to own very personal dilemmas, and who inform our all-too-human dilemma of sharing and serving as imperfect beings. Heroes who would help us see that it is the purity of our love that matters, not how gifted we are in love or how powerful we are so that our love has a wider radius. Ideally, we would feel it is all right for us to be imperfect in execution, all right to be a human being, all right to be confused about what to do and how—provided we are aligned with our calling and feel it in our hearts. Learning from these heroes, we would understand that a flourishing life is open to non-heroes too, just like us.

17. Hyde, *Gift*, xvii.
18. Otto, *Idea of the Holy*, 177–78.

PART II

Preparing for Big Decisions

5

Calling, or Purpose

Wouldn't it be nice to be one of Abraham Maslow's "self-actualizing people"?

"*All such people*," Maslow writes, in italics, "*are devoted to some task, call, vocation, beloved work ('outside themselves')*."[1] Notice those words: call, vocation, beloved work, and outside themselves. A similar concept is *purpose*, as in one's life purpose.

In one definition, purpose "refers to a long-term, forward-looking intention to accomplish aims that are both meaningful to the self and of consequence to the world beyond the self."[2] "Intention" means our *will* is key; this is not being a passive recipient. "Meaningful" suggests that the calling is based on our values and beliefs, which are the products of our upbringing and current contexts but are also subject to our active choice. And finally, "consequence" means that our purpose goes beyond our own well-being; even though it turns out that having a calling is correlated with one's well-being, that's not the point.

How can we realize or refurbish our calling or purpose?

"MY CALLING JUST BECAME EVIDENT"

For some people, this question is moot. They know their calling from an early age.

1. Maslow, *Farther Reaches*, 301.
2. Bronk and Mitchell, "Youth Purpose," 234.

Consider the great maker of stained-glass windows Rowan LeCompte. Here is how LeCompte recalled an experience he had in his early teens.

> I was passionately interested in architecture and in painting, and I could never decide which I wanted to do first. When I first saw the cathedral, however, by chance it was dazzling summer day with cool temperatures and brilliant sun. The building was half built. We walked up a set of concrete steps and across a great walk of wood to a big tin wall held up by vast beams of wood and then in through a door into darkness, but it wasn't darkness. There was a marvelous rose window floating in the dark, and I was inside a vast building, the like of which I had never seen or been in. It went up to an unthinkable height, and the air was filled with music because the organ was only one year old then and the organist was practicing, and he was playing Handel and I recognized it at once. But I did not recognize the building as anything I had ever seen before. It was a magic, marvelous, dim, ravishingly beautiful place. And I was stunned. Really, I was stunned. And I think of that as my second birthday, because it did change my life utterly and from that time on I was obsessed with it.[3]

When we see LeCompte's beautiful stained-glass windows in the National Cathedral in Washington—the first of which was commissioned when he was sixteen—and when we hear him describe kindness and love as his ideals, we are grateful that he found such a good and proper calling for him.

When he was an eight-year-old boy, the philosopher R. G. Collingwood came across a book of Immanuel Kant's in his father's library. Fascinated though confused, Collingwood felt a kind of calling.

> As I began reading it, my small form wedged between the bookcase and the table, I was attacked by a strange succession of emotions. First came an intense excitement. I felt that things of the highest importance were being said about matters of the utmost urgency: things which at all costs I must understand. Then, with a wave of indignation, came the discovery that I could not understand them. Disgraceful to confess, here was a book whose words were English and whose sentences were grammatical, but whose meaning baffled me. Then, third and last, came the strangest emotion of all. I felt that the contents of this book, although I could not understand it, were somehow my business: a matter personal to myself, or rather to some

---

3. LeCompte, interview with Scott Simon.

future self of my own . . . I felt as if a veil had been lifted and my destiny revealed.[4]

Other people, too, just seem to know to know when they are young that they should become a doctor or a painter or a nuclear physicist (or a conductor—see Box 3).

BOX 3. TANNHÄUSER DOES IT AGAIN

When he was only five, Andris Nelsons heard Richard Wagner's *Tannhäuser* live. "It had a hypnotic effect on me," he told Richard Morrison. "I was overwhelmed by the music. I cried when Tannhäuser died. I still think this was the biggest thing that happened in my childhood."[5]

He later explained to Harriet Gilbert the calling he received.

> Harriet Gilbert: I read somewhere, Andris, that it was while you were watching a Wagner opera at the tender age of five that you decided you wanted to become a conductor. Is that right?
>
> Andris Nelsons: Yes, you know it's true. I was five years old when my father took me to the opera house, and it was Wagner's Tannhäuser. I was so touched by this opera, and I was crying, and I was so so emotional after that. And interestingly enough, during the performance I was watching the conductor, and I was thinking, "Oh my God, it must be such a great responsibility. If he does something wrong, everything goes wrong, and it's his fault." So I was thinking, it must be great to be involved in the music so much as the conductor. That was subconsciously my dream. Someday I would like to become a conductor, not because of being you know in front of the people but because of being involved in music all the time, you know, from the first to the last bar.[6]

Or a scientist interested in tiny things. Dan Schechtman describes the early arrival of his calling.

---

4. Collingwood, *Autobiography*, 3.
5. Morrison, "Nelsons's Rapid Rise."
6. Nelsons, interview with Harriet Gilbert.

When I was 7 years old, my grandfather bought me an extraordinary present—a magnifying glass! It made me very happy and I started walking around the city of Ramat Gan (in Israel) with this magnifying glass. I looked at everything I could find—flowers, bugs, sand, and many other small things. During this process I fell in love with the world of small things. A few years later, when I was in the fifth grade, a microscope was delivered to our school. Week after week, I asked my teacher to bring the microscope to our class. Eventually he did, and he invited me to be the first to look through it. We looked at a leaf, and I could see the motion of the chlorophyll, a small molecule inside the leaf responsible for its green color. Since then I could not leave the microscope. Years later, during my studies at the Technion (Israel Institute of Technology), an exceptionally strong microscope arrived at our facility, called a transmission electron microscope (TEM). I fell in love with this microscope because it allowed me to realize my scientific curiosity for the world of small things. I soon specialized in operating this microscope, and by using it I discovered a new type of material which, many years later, earned me a Nobel prize.[7]

Or a Buddhist monk. On a long hike, a Bhutanese friend told me about his family. One son was in Florida studying to be a pilot. Another, thirteen years old, was a monk.

Already! I asked how he became a monk so young. To paraphrase his answer: his son began having spiritual experiences before he was ten. In a short while, the son recognized himself as the reincarnation of a revered monk from centuries ago. The family took the son to a monastery. This led to interviews with religious leaders, during which the son's knowledge gave to them clear evidence that he was in fact this reincarnation.

My friend pulled out a snapshot. There were he, his wife, and the two sons, big smiles, all in regular clothes. My friend said the boy can come home for a week every year.

What did my friend think of this?

"My son is as happy and fulfilled as can be" was the answer. And my friend was convinced that his son's calling is authentic—in fact, fated.

Sometimes people know early the *kind* of calling they want, without yet the specifics. As a girl, the author Annie Dillard devoured biographies of great men and women. She discerned a pattern that became her goal. "This was life itself: the big task. Nothing exhilarated me more than the idea of a life dedicated to a monumental worthwhile task." She carried "a secret

7. Schechtman, "Quasi-Crystal, Not Quasi-Scientist."

knowledge, a secret joy, and a secret hope: There is a life worth living where history is still taking place; there are ideas worth dying for, and circumstances where courage is still prized. This life could be found and joined, like the Resistance."[8]

WHAT IF YOU DON'T KNOW YOUR CALLING?

If you are not like these lucky souls, how can you discover your calling? One idea is to sit down, think hard, and figure it out.

Howard Raiffa, one of the pioneers of decision theory, told a story about the late 1960s, a time of social upheaval and uncertainty about what really mattered. One of Raiffa's students decided to write his senior honors thesis on the topic, "What I Should Do after Graduation." The student employed decision theory to analyze his options. He laid out every contingency pertaining to every choice. He assigned a numerical value to each possible outcome. Then he calculated which path had the highest expected utility for him. This was the calling he should follow.

The answer shocked the student. His analysis concluded that he should join the army.

During the Vietnam War, this was certainly not the usual answer. Something, the bewildered student concluded, is wrong with decision theory. He immediately consulted Professor Raiffa. How, he asked, could this mathematical analysis of his life choices have produced such a bizarre result?

Raiffa went back to the beginning. What did the student value, and how much compared with other things? The student had found it uncomfortable to try to list all the so-called attributes of his utility function—and then to try to trade them off against one other. But he tried again, and he and Raiffa reviewed the list one by one. Suddenly, the student lit up.

"I see what I forgot," he exclaimed. "I left out my love life!"

This is not an omission I would expect many college seniors to make. But the point is that when you think about the future, it is hard to keep in mind all the things that matter.

Most formal techniques for analyzing choice assume that the things you value are given. But these may be precisely what you need to discover. What values should you pursue? What calling should you follow? You probably can't find out by writing a senior thesis. You probably can't reason your way to a satisfying answer. Instead, you may need to try out different callings and see how they feel.

8. Dillard, *Three by Annie Dillard*, 451.

This is relevant for people of all ages. The Halftime seminars based on the work of Bob Buford[9] are designed for people who have already achieved great things, usually in business. They have money now; their résumés are full of did-this, hit-that-key-performance-indicator. But an upheaval arrives. They sense that there must be a deeper purpose to their lives. In workshops that include self-exploration and exposure to heroes, participants think anew about their callings, insights, and abilities to share and serve.

Whatever your age, the point is not discovering some hidden essence of who you are. Over time and experience, we develop values as well as capabilities. You *become* someone different in terms of both what you want and what you can do.[10]

FIVE CATEGORIES OF CALLINGS

It's a truism that experience is the great teacher, but I like that word *experiment*. It emphasizes that learning from experience need not be haphazard. We can plan our experiences and evaluate them.

How might you think about experimenting to discover and develop your calling? As a warm-up exercise, let's consider five categories of callings. Under each of the five, a large variety of specific callings reside. But thinking about the big categories may be a useful start.

1. Make Yourself Happy

The first category relates to one's own happiness and fulfillment. If someone asks you why you are doing thus-and-so with your life, the appropriate answer is "Because it makes me happy." This calling is also familiar from what you'll hear some parents say about their children. "I don't care what they do, as long as it makes them happy."

But what will make you happy, or happiest? The philosopher Moritz Schlick argues persuasively that both *pleasures* and *goal-directed accomplishments* fade quickly as sources of happiness. Instead, you should focus on things that, to you, matter for their own sake. Because philosophers

---

9. https://halftimeinstitute.org/programs/.

10. For a valuable, example-laden analysis of the difference between Raiffa-style decision analysis and deciding whom to become, see Callard, *Aspiration*, especially chapter 1. She describes aspiration as both a process of value acquisition and a process of becoming a certain kind of person. Aspirants, like you and me when we ponder whom to become, are engaged in a kind of self-making, self-shaping, or self-creation.

seem so dour, it may surprise you how Schlick characterizes these things: not *work* but *play*.

To be happy, "we must seek for *activities* which carry their own purpose and value within them, independently of any extraneous goals; activities, therefore, which are not work, in the philosophical sense of the word."[11]

"Play, as we see it, is any activity which takes place entirely for its own sake, independently of its effects and consequences. There is nothing to stop these effects from being of a useful or valuable kind. If they are, so much the better; the action still remains play, since it already bears its own value within itself."[12]

> The richest blessings flow from the work that is engendered as the child of its creator's happy mood, and in free play, without any anxious concern for its effects . . . The tilling of the fields, the weaving of fabrics, the cobbling of shoes, can all become play, and may take on the character of artistic acts. Nor is it even so uncommon for a man to take so much pleasure in such activities, that he forgets the purpose of them. Every true craftsman can experience in his own case this transformation of the means into an end-in-itself, which can take place with almost any activity, and which makes the product into a work of art. It is the joy in sheer creation, the dedication to the activity, the absorption in the movement, which transforms work into play.[13]

Note the humble examples here. The psychologists Bryan J. Dik and Ryan Duffy show how "almost any kind of occupation can offer any one of us a sense of calling. Regardless of where we are in our careers, we can all find joy and meaning in the work we do, from the construction zone flagger who keeps his crew safe to the corporate executive who believes that her company's products will change the world."[14]

A related idea is *flow*, defined as "a state in which people are so involved in an activity that nothing else seems to matter; the experience is so enjoyable that people will continue to do it even at great cost, for the sheer sake of doing it."[15]

To be happy, find what meaningful play is for you. Find what gives you flow.

11. Schlick, "Meaning of Life," 116.

12. Schlick, "Meaning of Life," 115–16.

13. Schlick, "Meaning of Life," 117.

14. Dik and Duffy, *Job a Calling*, cover.

15. Csikszentmihalyi, *Flow*, 4.

2. Altruism, or Making Others Happy

Contrast a second basic calling, altruism. Here the idea is to increase everyone's happiness, not just your own. You should choose a life that contributes to the greatest good for the greatest number—to use a familiar formulation that is, strictly speaking, impossible—and you should do so even if some other path would leave you better off.

Attention: it turns out not to be so easy to say what makes humankind happier.

3. Uncover the Truth

A third basic value might be called scientific. The goal here is not to make yourself or others happy, but rather to seek and to attain truth. Forget about serving yourself or serving others. No great scientist, advises Max Weber, "has ever done anything but serve his work and only his work."[16]

4. Create Art

A fourth calling is artistic. The idea here is to create something authentic and uniquely yours. "Within the world of art," writes the philosopher Stanley Cavell, "one makes one's own dangers, takes one's chances—and one speaks of its objects at such moments in terms of tension, problem, imbalance, necessity, shock, surprise."[17] Notice that Cavell does not include happiness, altruism, or truth among the objects of art.

5. Engage with Ultimate Reality

Finally, a fifth basic value might be called religious or spiritual. Describing the goal here is difficult. One may speak of trying to engage infinity, or ultimate reality, or God. The psychoanalyst Erik Erikson created the category of *homo religious* to characterize the person "who looks through the historical parade of cultures and civilizations, styles, and isms which provide most of us with a glorious and yet miserably fragile sense of immortal identity, defined status, and collective grandeur and faces the central truth of nothingness—and, *mirabile dictu*, gains power from it."[18]

16. Weber, "Science as a Vocation," 137.
17. Cavell, *Must We Mean*, 199.
18. Erikson, *Gandhi's Truth*, 399.

WHICH CALLINGS FOR YOU?

We should immediately admit that these five categories are neither exhaustive nor exclusive. They do not necessarily conflict. On the other hand, these diverse callings do not automatically overlap. Schlick noted that your play may end up helping others, though that is not play's purpose.

You may not know which calling should be yours. How might you find out?

My suggestion is that you can't do it in your armchair. You need experience. So, go ahead and get experience in the most efficient fashion: experiment. Make a willful effort to put yourself in circumstances—and in the frame of mind—where you can test alternative ways of valuing the world. Be an experimenter—with your own life.[19]

For example, for the first calling of your own happiness, you might try out Nietzsche's advice:

> This is the most effective way:—to let the youthful soul look back on life with the question, "What hast thou up to now truly loved, what has drawn thy soul upward, mastered it and blessed it too?" Set up these things that thou hast honoured before thee, and, maybe, they will show thee, in their being and their order, a law which is the fundamental law of thine own self. Compare these objects, consider how one completes and broadens and transcends and explains another, how they form a ladder on which thou hast all the time been climbing to thy self: for thy true being lies not deeply hidden in thee, but an infinite height above thee, or at least above that which thou dost commonly take to be thyself.[20]

You might test your altruistic values by placing yourself in an impoverished setting where you define your calling as helping those around you. This requires that you first listen to and learn from them.

You might experiment with your artistic side and devote yourself painting or sculpting or composing. Take a pottery class. Then experiment with, say, six hours a day of throwing pots.

To explore a religious dimension, you might try spending hours a day in prayer and meditation. In J. D. Salinger's novel *Franny and Zoey*,

---

19. Friedrich Nietzsche proclaimed and exhorted "philosophers of the future" who "will be men of experiments. By the name with which I ventured to baptize them, I have already expressly emphasized their attempting and their love of attempting is this because, as critics in body and soul, they will love to make use of experiments in a new, and perhaps wider and more dangerous sense." Nietzsche, *Beyond Good and Evil*, §210.

20. Nietzsche, "Schopenhauer as Educator," 107.

twenty-year-old Franny is experiencing upheaval. She happens upon the "Jesus Prayer" in a nineteenth-century Russian Orthodox book called *The Way of a Pilgrim*. The Jesus Prayer is short: "Lord Jesus, son of God, have mercy on me, a sinner." What attracts Franny, a Jew, is not its substance but its use. It is supposed to be said continually. Breathe in, "Lord Jesus, son of God." Breathe out, "Have mercy on me, a sinner." Franny decides to experiment with constant prayer. So did the pilgrim in the book, first for minutes at a time, then for hours. Sometimes he attained bliss, that sought-for union with the divine. But he didn't feel holy for all that. His first line in *The Way of a Pilgrim* is this: "By the grace of God I am a Christian man, by my own actions a great sinner, and by calling a homeless wanderer of the humblest origins, roaming from place to place."[21]

Martin Luther wrote of the need to experiment. "Christian faith has appeared to many an easy thing; nay, not a few even reckon it among the social virtues, as it were; and this they do because they have not made proof of it experimentally, and have never tasted of what efficacy it is. For it is not possible for any man to write well about it, or to understand well what is rightly written, who has not at some time tasted of its spirit, under the pressure of tribulation; while he who has tasted of it, even to a very small extent, can never write, speak, think, or hear about it sufficiently."[22]

GESTATION

If you undertake such experiments with your life, you might expect several things to happen. It will probably take time for an answer to emerge for you. The process may be likened to pregnancy. After a gestation period, a clarification of your deepest values, even that feeling of wholeness you have been looking for, may emerge, naturally.

If you are fortunate, your calling and insight may combine a personal problem—*your* personal problem—with a problem outside yourself, in historical time. Such a combination, Erik Erikson observed, distinguished the lives of Luther, Darwin, Freud, and Gandhi—and, I believe, Erikson himself. Each of them tacked back and forth between their individual contradiction and the world's version of that contradiction—and doing so sustained the passion that enabled them to change the world.[23]

21. *Way of a Pilgrim*, 1.

22. Luther, "Concerning Christian Liberty," 344–45.

23. Erikson, "Autobiographic Notes." See also Erikson, *Gandhi's Truth* and *Young Man Luther*.

In none of their cases, Erikson's research discovered, did their calling come simply by seeking it. The calling arrived during a time of what Erikson labels a "moratorium," after a period of preparation and an upheaval. Darwin left the university behind on a boat trip around the world. Gandhi departed from his legal studies in London, where he had occasionally dressed in a top hat and gloves, to work with the poor in South Africa. Luther had a personal crisis just as he was about to become a Catholic priest, and his moratorium was a time of protected reflection under a sympathetic mentor.

You too may need a moratorium. Finding a calling does require preparation—it is not passive. But it is not something one does simply by pursuing a degree or taking a particular job.

In fact, finding your calling may even be hindered by trying too hard or too soon to define it. William James compared the process to incubation: "When the new center of personal energy has been subconsciously incubated so long as to be just ready to open into flower, 'hands off' is the only word for us, it must burst forth unaided."[24]

Thich Nhat Hanh, considered by some of his followers to be a "Living Buddha," expressed a similar idea: "Sitting and looking deeply into your body, your consciousness, and your mental states is like being a mother hen covering her eggs. One day insight will be born like a baby chick."[25] Along the way, accidents made good, even what the philosopher Willard V. Quine called "happy confusions," turn out to be welcome, in your life and in biological evolution.[26] Friedrich Nietzsche concurs (see Box 4).

So, in times of upheaval or transition, if you don't know what to do with your life, take heart. You are not certain exactly what you value or should value—and that's all right, whatever your age. To find your calling, don't just think about it. Experiment.

Seek guidance from exemplars in particular areas you study or work. And, beyond your particular areas now, get acquainted with the heroes of legend, history, and everyday life—people whose struggles and callings resonate with your own.

24. James, *Varieties of Religious Experience*, 210.

25. Nhat Hanh, *Living Buddha*, 49.

26. "Happy confusions are frequent in biological evolution: a disused organ or accidental growth becomes diverted in a later generation, by natural selection, to a vital new use. Boons, like people, are to be valued for themselves and not for their origins. Serendipity and opportunism are laws of nature." Quine, *Stimulus to Science*, 28–29.

BOX 4. "I DON'T HAVE A CLUE"

One evening when she was a fifteen-year-old high school freshman, our daughter Kristen talked about the pressures of trying to excel at high levels in many things. She was playing volleyball. She also loved her singing and her studies. And yet, she felt she lacked a calling or purpose. Some of her friends seemed to know exactly what they wanted and what they should become.

"They ask me what I'm going to do, where I want to go to college. I don't have a clue."

I got up and fetched the laptop. I read to Kristen some examples of folks who just knew what they would be and then noted that most of us aren't like that. What should we do?

These words of Friedrich Nietzsche's struck Kristen.

> To become what one is, one must not have the faintest notion of *what* one is. From this point of view even the *blunders* of life have their own meaning and value—the occasional side roads and wrong roads, the delays, "modesties," seriousness wasted on tasks that are remote from *the* task. All this can express great prudence, even the supreme prudence: where *nosce te ipsum* [know thyself] would be the recipe for ruin, forgetting oneself, *misunderstanding* oneself . . . become reason itself . . .
>
> So many dangers that the instinct comes too soon to "understand itself." Meanwhile the organizing "idea" that is destined to rule keeps growing deep down—it begins to command; slowly it leads us *back* from side roads and wrong roads; it prepares "single" qualities and fitnesses that will one day prove to be indispensable as means toward a whole—one by one, it trains all *servient* capacities before giving any hint of the dominant task, "goal," "aim," or "meaning."[27]

Kristen got a big aha!: she didn't have to try to figure out right now what her passion is, or even who she is. Over time, in due time, she should experiment.

"Dad, would you send that passage of Nietzsche's to me?"

I did, and that night Nietzsche's first sentence was a text box on her Facebook main page.

---

27. Nietzsche, *Ecce Homo*, 710.

If you are lucky in your experimentation, you may experience some-thing akin to falling in love. To cite Abraham Maslow once more:

> I hesitate to call this simply "purposefulness" because that may imply that it happens only out of will, purpose, decision, or calculation, and doesn't give enough weight to the subjective feeling of being swept along, of willing and eager surrender, or yielding to fate and happily embracing it at the same time. Ideally, one also *discovers* one's fate; it is not only made or con-structed or decided upon. It is recognized as if one had been unwittingly waiting for it . . .
>
> The best way to communicate these feelings to someone who doesn't intuitively, directly understand them is to use as a model "falling in love." This is clearly different from doing one's duty, or doing what is sensible and logical. And clearly also "will," if mentioned at all, is used in a very special sense. And when two people love each other fully, then each one knows what it feels like to be a magnet and what it feels like to be iron filings, and what it feels like to be both simultaneously.[28]

---

28. Maslow, *Farther Reaches*, 303.

6

Big Insights

An exuberant advertisement for financial software once described the feeling of having an insight. The software's user sees raw data from the stock market instantly transformed into insights.

> This is what we call the "Ah-hah! Factor."
>
> As in "Ah-hah! That stock is way undervalued."
>
> Or, "Ah-hah! We've got a terrible portfolio balance here."
>
> Or, "Ah-hah! The trend suggests a trend in XYZ company's stock prices by late spring."
>
> Or, "Ah-hah! We better get out of this while we still have our shirts."
>
> Ah-hah! is the sudden glow of insight. The hair on the back of your neck that tells you you're on to something that no one else has seen yet.
>
> It's the difference between a very informed buy-sell decision and a not-so-hot one.

One dictionary defines insight as "a clear understanding of the inner nature of some specific thing." But the "ah-hah!" of the software ad captures an important nuance. An insight surprises us, grabs us, satisfies us. Arthur Koestler went so far as to characterize three of mankind's most basic reactions as:

> "Ah!—That feels good!"
> "Aha!—That makes sense!"
> "Haha!—That's funny!"

Which itself may or may not be an insight.[1]

BIG INSIGHTS

The second step in the hero's path involves a big insight. But what are "big insights"? Where do insights came from? What can they become?

Let's begin with a related concept in psychology, *meaningfulness*. Viktor Frankl once noticed that people don't give up because they are unhappy but because their lives seem to them to lack meaning. But what does *meaning* mean? It sounds easy till you think about it, and psychologists themselves have foundered over a general definition.[2] One workable idea separates calling and purpose, which are subjective and aspirational, from meaning, which is cognitive and descriptive. Meaning is a sense of coherence between people's beliefs and their perceptions of the world around them, coupled with the perception that the world is orderly and not chaotic.

In this chapter, we consider a similar cognitive idea. A big insight is a cognitive model or theory that suddenly makes sense of a series of puzzles in our world, perhaps also in ourselves. Most big insights are only tangentially related to concerns about the meaningfulness of our lives or of life itself.

Consider the example of the philosopher Thomas Kuhn. When he first studied Aristotle, Kuhn was astonished by how clumsy, how weird, were Aristotle's statements about the theory of motion, in contrast to his subtlety and lasting wisdom in matters of morality. How could this be?

After pondering this for a long time, Kuhn was suddenly struck by a big insight. You must read Aristotle as if you are inside his time and place, with empathy toward that whole way of looking at the world. What had seemed absurd now made sense. Science in Aristotle's time talked about the world differently. "Qualities" and "changes in qualities" were their preoccupation. "Experiments" for them were inside one's head or in everyday experience. (Random question: just like philosophers today?)

Kuhn got a big aha! "When reading the works of an important thinker, look first for the apparent absurdities in the text and ask yourself how a sensible person could have written them. When you find an answer . . . then you may find that more central passages, ones you previously thought you understood, have changed their meaning."[3] Before dismissing someone's views or theories—or for that matter, before accepting them—try to understand where they are coming from. These points resonate more generally. In

1. Koestler, *Act of Creation*.
2. Martela and Steger, "Three Meanings."
3. Kuhn, *Essential Tension*, xii.

a world of diverse peoples, ideologies, religions, and the like, it is important for understanding what they say and do to try to inhabit their worlds and worldviews.

This big insight was a foundation for Kuhn's classic book, *The Structure of Scientific Revolutions*. Science and scientific theories depend on the time and place. "Like the choice between competing political institutions," Kuhn wrote, "that between competing [scientific] paradigms proves to be a choice between incompatible norms of community life . . . Each group uses its own paradigm to argue in that paradigm's defense."[4] And forget about so-called objective truth: "In these matters," Kuhn noted, "neither proof nor error is at issue. The transfer of allegiance from paradigm to paradigm is a conversion experience that cannot be forced."[5]

The Structure of Scientific Revolutions has raised hopes and hackles far outside the history and philosophy of science. Extreme Kuhnians apply his big insight more generally. Facts are in the eyes of the beholder, they say; so are truth and progress.

EXAMPLES OF BIG INSIGHTS

Later in this chapter we will return to Kuhn, but now let's look at some other big ahas. Let's consider a few insights that for some people suddenly make sense of a range of puzzles or paradoxes and generate novel ways to understand the world. Do they have common features? And without proper management on our part, might the big ahas soon cease to be playful and useful, and start to be counterproductive?

We'll explore these questions by examining four big insights from different fields: economics, sociology, religion, and clinical psychology. In the spirit of playful insight enjoyment, I will condense into each big aha! packages of insights, even populations of insights, and I will pretend that only one, albeit large, insight resides in each category. This simplification is nowhere more apparent than in discussing "the" elementary economic insight.

The Economic Insight

The movie mogul Samuel Goldwyn once discussed making a film with George Bernard Shaw. Goldwyn elaborated on the joys of pure art and the

---

4. Kuhn, *Structure of Scientific Revolutions*, 94.

5. Kuhn, *Structure of Scientific Revolutions*, 151.

importance of great movies. After this had continued for some time, Shaw became impatient.

"Well, Mr. Goldwyn," Shaw declared, "there is not much use in going on. There is this difference between you and me: You are only interested in art, and I am only interested in money."[6]

What ensued is not recorded. Maybe Goldwyn saw nothing more than rudeness and responded with something unprintable. Or maybe Goldwyn later had a big insight. Maybe Shaw's joke had a serious point. Maybe Shaw really did only care about money, and for that matter, Goldwyn may have been prodded to think, maybe that's all anyone cared about. To dress the point, maybe all everybody did was maximize their profits.

If Goldwyn entertained such a notion, he was close to what might be called the elementary economic insight. Each person has a bunch of tastes and capabilities. Each invests their efforts and resources in one or another activity. What the person decides to do is determined by the relative profitability of the various activities. People are seen as if they are maximizing net utility as assessed according to their own tastes, given their capabilities and the uncertain rewards for each available activity.

If you have the economic insight, you calculate at the margin,[7] for that is where economics shows that maximizing calculations should take place. You draw implications for people, firms, and governments. For example, competitive prices should be set equal to marginal costs: otherwise, prices are "distorted" and aggregate output will not be "optimal." You say that exchange rates and tariffs and taxes and tolls should be set in a similar way: the marginal social cost should equal the marginal social benefit. Along with each person's endowments and tastes, the incentives they face take center stage. How a maximizer behaves is importantly explained by the incentive structure.

As abstract and simple as this insight may be, once you have it, it flies everywhere. Someone may talk about how redistributing incomes may be fairer than what we have now. If you have the economic insight, you can't help but ask how the redistribution will affect incentives. How will the purportedly fairer system affect the relative profitability of various activities and therefore affect, after people maximize away, the resulting total amount of income and its distribution?

Or suppose someone else says that rents should be controlled so that poor people can have affordable housing. During a pandemic or a

6. For various versions of Shaw's remark, see the Quote Investigator's report: http://quoteinvestigator.com/2013/03/30/art-money/#more-5828.

7. Think of the margin as the edge from which a choice is to be made. A choice at the margin is a decision to do a little more or a little less of something.

depression, the state should mandate a moratorium on paying rent. As a person with the elementary economic insight, you will wonder about the resulting incentives for landlords—and you may forecast that with rent control there will less and poorer quality housing in the long run.

The economist's insight may creep, or indeed sprint, into domains beyond economics. If you are fond of insects, you may find that the behavior of ants or bees can be understood as maximizing the colony's or hive's chances of survival. Closer to home, it may seem to you that calculations of costs and benefits serve to summarize your child's decision to obey you without whining or your own decision to watch TV tonight instead of reading that book you've been meaning to. You may even start to think of altruism with the economic insight. Isn't there an optimal degree of altruism where one should do something that increases the welfare of another provided that it doesn't cost too much in foregone welfare of one's own?

The elementary economic insight has psychological side effects. Your predictions about rent control can be advanced without knowing the details of a particular housing system, and you don't need to study philosophy to be able to make some arresting points about fairness and altruism. You may come to think that having this insight excuses you from the burdensome study of many details and of other big insights. This insight may start to seem self-sufficient.

And you may become frustrated with those who don't share the elementary economic insight. As Joan Robinson said, "You only realize that it's not common sense when you start to argue with someone who doesn't have it."

On the other hand, this exclusivity may help make it feel like a big insight. Others—the uninitiated, including you until you experienced the aha!—don't get it. It's not common sense; it's even counterintuitive. You may be excused for feeling proud of having the insight, if not for what often goes along with that feeling: disdain for those who do not have it.

There is a fairly standard method for transferring this insight to others. It takes about a semester in a classroom, though this method is not always successful. You need to put the initiates in the mood to think abstractly, get them to make some assumptions, such as that there are these markets with identical people and products and everybody knows everything, and suddenly the price goes up and . . . then they too may say "aha!" If they do, it will make you happy.

Some people specialize in the economic insight. Academic economics has benefits, but its practical relevance is often disappointing. Sometimes proving the insight's simplest ahas becomes an end in itself. For example, research papers may strive mightily to prove that the sign of the relationship between price and quantity supplied is positive in industry X, just as the elementary economic insight says it should be. This qualitative result may be a long way from practical application, but fellow holders of the insight will be heartened.

Nonetheless, the elementary economic insight has practical applications, or gets applied. The British economist David Henderson and the American economist Paul Krugman (among others) have lamented that policies are so often influenced by the economic arguments, not of academicians or specialists, but of "do-it-yourself economists" and "cranks."

"Unfortunately," lamented *The Economist* in a review of the state of economics, "it is these primitive models, rather than their sophisticated descendants, that often exert the most influence over the world of policy and practice . . . These basic models are also influential because of their simplicity. Faced with the 'blooming, buzzing confusion' of the real world, policymakers often fall back on the highest-order principles and the broadest presumptions."[8]

In this handyman sense, the elementary economic insight slides into a free-market ideology of public and social policy. As in other ideologies, there are villains and promised lands. Here the enemies are those that distort prices from the optimal marginal equivalencies or interfere with individual maximizing in the marketplace. These villains include bureaucratic controls, monopolies, big business and big labor and big media, and all intrusions on individual choice. To be promoted are competition and incentives; to be avoided are government interference and shirking. Utopia is attained when individuals maximize their self-interests. Distrust those who say that people will work hard for the state or ideology or art. Remember, all George Bernard Shaw cared about was money.

The economic insight has degenerate forms. From an astonishingly simple recasting of reality that helps one to see what one had not seen, the insight may come to replace reality. The assumptions of competitive microeconomics? They are poor approximations of reality. People and products are not identical, and people are not perfectly informed. In such circumstances we cannot count on pure competition to deliver the right incentives. (Some of the best economists have proved that statement.)

Sometimes the elementary insight fails in another way. In experimental economics, an efficient equilibrium is often reached even with only a few, ill-informed, incompletely rational actors in the market. In his Nobel Prize lecture, Vernon Smith observed, "The unexpectedly weak conditions under which the results obtain are good news for market performance, but not

8. "Other-Worldly Philosophers," 67.

such good news for the scientific community because it demonstrates that we do not understand why markets work the way they do."[9]

And remember those preferences we said people had. Where do they come from? Are they all equally worthy? Do values enter here? Might those values be non-individualistic? Plausible answers to these questions leave the simplest version of the economic insight in the dust. The implications of the simplest economic insight can often be shown by more careful thinking to be wrong. And the economic insight can degenerate into a pernicious ideology.

A MORPHOLOGY OF INSIGHTS?

As I reflected on these points about the economic insight, I began to wonder if other big ahas follow a similar pattern.

What pattern? First, a sudden insight in the sense of "immediate and clear learning that takes place without recourse to overt trial-and-error behavior"—one of the definitions in *Webster's Unabridged Dictionary*—clarifies a puzzle and causes delight. Then one sees that the insight applies over a surprising range. The scope of a big insight comes to seem boundless, in the sense of leading to a partial, qualitative, non-obvious understanding of many phenomena.

The insight then has psychological side effects. One tends to forget the "partial" and "qualitative" aspects of the understanding attained and instead tends to glory in what is "non-obvious" to others. Reductionism lurks: one may think it unnecessary to learn the specifics of a situation or to master other insights. One may become exasperated with those who do not have the insight. This frustration may coexist with a sense of superiority and with a feeling of solidarity with fellow insight-holders. A big insight breeds a community of believers. The methods for conveying the aha! should be standard but exacting: possessing a big insight is exclusive but not unique.

Big insights are taken up academically. This leads to intricate studies that reinforce the basic lessons of the insight but have little practical value. For insight-holders, however, the studies are existentially satisfying.

Big insights get applied, often far afield. Usually, the appliers are not distinguished academicians but purveyors of simplification. Often their applications can be shown by masters of the insight to be invalid.

---

9. Smith, "Constructivist and Ecological Rationality," 468n.

In the course of all this, a big insight that began as an illuminator of reality may turn out, in certain hands, to shroud reality. Insight ends up as ideology.[10]

How well does this morphology apply to other big insights? Consider a sociological antidote to the economic insight.

The Marxist Insight

Behind the appearances of economic and political life are the interests of groups, especially of economic classes. These interests are the ultimate forces of society. If someone says, "We are doing this because it is right or just or socially optimal or the will of Allah," the person with the elementary Marxist insight knows better. They are doing it because it is in the interest of their class. Because whatever class is in power will make all policy choices on its own behalf, the only way to have change is to change the class in power.

If you have this insight, you gain a sudden sophistication, even cynicism. Take the current debate over public schools. Others discuss the pros and cons of various programs to improve learning in schools. You see things differently. Schools are not primarily about cognitive skills but about class warfare: they are designed to teach future workers to be punctual, to accept the current social system, and to obey authority. You see the real issue as the socialization of the next generation of workers.

Or take foreign aid. The bourgeois debate deals with such questions as the effectiveness of aid strategies in promoting growth and equity. You realize the real question in the background must be one of classes, both across and within nations. So, the real purpose of foreign aid must be to support the ruling classes' domination of international and domestic markets and politics. The issue is how alternative aid strategies fulfill that objective—and how this harms the classes not in power.

Class interests have their own dynamic. Depending on the state of technology and the level of "development," certain classes will come to the fore in a predictable dialectic. (The time of the proletariat is coming.) Class interests dominate even science. Sure, scientists talk about pursuing truth. But if you have the Marxist insight, you know that truth is not absolute but can only be defined in terms of class interests. Kuhnians enter here: the

---

10. Ideology in the negative senses of "theorizing of a visionary or impractical nature" (one definition in *The Random House Dictionary of the English Language*) and "an extremist sociopolitical program or philosophy constructed wholly or in part on factitious or hypothetical ideational bases" (one definition in *Webster's Unabridged Dictionary*).

history of science shows that the paradigms that have guided scientists like so many mice in a maze are those imposed by the prevailing class-dominated ideology.

The purveyor of the Marxist insight distrusts positivism, individualism, and any static theory of preferences and capabilities. Positivism says that there is a truth out there in value-free, empirical space and time. Nonsense. According to the Marxist insight, nothing is value free because nothing in this world exists except in a world of classes. Individualism is a charade. As a description it is simply inaccurate, and as a goal it is a reactionary bourgeois trick to keep the exploited classes' minds off their real problems. Static theories—that is, theories that ignore dialectics—miss the heart of the problem, the class-based generation of preferences and capabilities. (The economic insight, especially, is attacked on this score.)

The Marxist insight conveys other benefits. It undercuts the usual debates—also, therefore, the importance of many of the usual facts and tools of analysis. It may consequently seem to you unnecessary to master the facts. Don't miss the forest for the trees. Raise consciousness and later we can worry about Robert Dahl's question, "After the revolution?"[11] And there's no need to master the usual analytical tools; the point is to uncover their hidden, nefarious, class-based assumptions. Having this big insight is intellectually economical.

You may also feel superior. Those who do not have the Marxist insight are naïve believers in appearances. Or they are reactionaries, the selfish upholders of the existing order and perpetrators of the systematic bourgeois campaign to cast everything in other terms than it really is. You may tend to apply terms like "systemic" and "radical" to your own way of thinking and analyzing social issues, saving for those without your insight such terms as "superficial" and "reformist." You may alternately feel proud of emphasizing the value dimensions of seemingly neutral approaches (thereby undercutting the technocrats) and of being a thoroughgoing materialist (thereby undercutting the moralists).

You may be frustrated with non-Marxists, but the fact that not everybody shares the insight also sets your worldview apart. It is a bond between you and your fellow insight-holders, creating solidarity despite your possibly different class backgrounds.

The Marxist insight can be conveyed. A main device is to show people that things are not what they appear. History is a main tool. (Marxist sociologists and economists tend toward the historical wings of their disciplines.) "You have been taught that the reason for the American Revolution

11. Dahl, *After the Revolution?*

was this, but look how this other version of the story makes more sense." Particularly subject to the insight's persuasion are those not doing well in the bourgeois world. It may be refreshing to know that the reason one is not succeeding is ultimately someone else's fault—more precisely, one's unjust exploitation by the class that is succeeding.

If you are bitten by the elementary Marxist insight, you may become an academic Marxist. Often this involves research to demonstrate that a historical event or a current process is qualitatively consistent with the idea that classes matter or that ruling classes tend to perpetuate their own interests. Usually this finding is a long way from prescriptive relevance and practical application, even in a Marxist nation.

But the Marxist insight gets applied. Class interests (workers, farmers, the poor) are the interests deserving attention. Their interests are served by "structural changes": controlling markets, inculcating (particular sorts of) values in education, and redistributing wealth. The enemies are laissez faire, individualism, religion (an opiate), and the bourgeois social order.

The Marxist insight has its degenerate forms, its lumpen Marxists. It sometimes stimulates a sophomoric negativism. "You can't separate facts from values . . . You can't talk about this problem without talking about the whole system . . . You can't talk about a tool of analysis without analyzing how it will be used and misused." It is not that such declarations are wrong but that they can become excuses for nihilism and escapes from details, subtlety, and hard work. The Marxist insight can slide into paranoia. Nothing is what it seems; someone else is always to blame for your problems or society's; there is always a conflict of interests. If a minority group is disadvantaged, it must be because a majority group benefits.

The Marxist insight in its degenerate forms collapses people into classes. It ignores individual differences and underemphasizes individual incentives. In its emphasis on conflict and the heavy swishing of a Hegelian dialectic, it seems to leave little room for compassion, cooperation, or love.

The Protestant Insight

Let us next examine a very different sort of insight and see how well our pattern of big insights holds.

Three key elements of Protestant insight are the presence of God as the creator of the world and of man in his image, the presence of evil in the world and in each of us, and the presence of love as the principle of redemption and restoration. If you have this insight, it may have come in this way:

"God loves me—awful me, evil me!" This big aha! can make you reframe your world.

Worldly striving for fame and fortune has been condemned by all the philosophers, even pagans; the Protestant insight says that it is equally fruitless to strive to achieve your salvation by doing good. No matter how much good you do, it is infinitely short of God's perfect good. Sinfulness and evil—to use two venerable concepts—are fundamental in every person and fundamental to you. Another way to put it: we all experience brokenness. According to the elementary Protestant insight, you need to remake how and why you live, going beyond what you do. In this remaking, that God loves you is your joy, as well as your example of how and why.

You may apply the insight more broadly. Just as your own evil will not be overcome by getting that job, writing that book, helping that person, or trying harder, so the world's evil will not be overcome by democracy or communism, by free markets or social welfare, by better education or better health care or better prisons. Evil in the world and in each of us can only be transcended through love—God's love and, thank God, sometimes our love as well.

If you have this insight, what seems important to others may seem trivial to you. Their preoccupations, their fields of study, the details of the question at hand: all may seem devoid of meaning compared with your infinite concerns. You may therefore feel safe in ignoring their worries, fields, and details. Indeed, these other people may exasperate you. What seems obvious to you—what really matters and what is superficial—evades them. They don't get it—they ask how you know God created the world, why the world is evil, indeed what it means to say, "God loves you." To those without the insight, Christianity's great mysteries—such as God becoming man, the virgin birth, the Trinity, and the resurrection—seem simply absurd. "Sure, love's great," they may say, "but not all the rest of that stuff."

But then again, if everyone had it, it wouldn't be a big insight. You may subconsciously feel even luckier because you have been blessed with the insight in a world of nonbelievers. If you are aware of this pride, you probably hope that you avoid its frequent companion, a disparaging attitude toward those who aren't insight-holders. You hope to remember that we are sinners all.

There are ways of conveying the Protestant insight to others. Religious services and "revivals" can propel conversion and recommitment. Christians of various stripes have developed processes for the inculcation and refurbishment of insight, such as St. Francis of Assisi's retreats or E. Stanley Jones's "round-table conferences" and "ashrams" in India. More often the insight is conveyed by example (as Jesus conveyed it), which sparks curiosity in others and then leads to a personal relationship in the context of which another person may understand the insight and give it a try. Studies show that the lower classes are overrepresented among the true believers: those most prone to adopt an otherworldly insight are those who in the present world fare less well.

Some Christians become academicians. Many theologians and professors of religion are so fascinated by the insight that they want to trace its origins, explicate its parables, venerate its saints. Theirs is not the task of applying the insight to present problems.

Yet the Protestant insight gets applied, often in surprising and sometimes in distressing ways. One of its glories is that it enables people to believe that life is not meaningless or random as some scientists seem to imply, nor ultimately materialist as the mass media seem to want us to profess. But this belief leads some of those with the Protestant insight to find enemies who need defeating: scientists who posit evolutionary doctrines or people that propagate humanist perspectives. The view may be taken further. If one is only saved from evil by having the insight, then we had better make sure everyone has the insight, like it or not. Those who do have it should be in charge of the state. They should decide what its schools teach, whether abortions are allowed, and even how foreign policy should deal with holy lands.

The Protestant insight can degenerate into its own dogmatism. The enemy of the instrumental view of life, it can become instrumental: believe this and you will be saved; don't and you will spend eternity in uncomfortable surroundings. From the source of joy and grace in God's love, the Protestant insight can become the smug and loveless conviction that we are right and they, those godless ones, are wrong.

The Process Insight

A fourth big insight is perhaps less familiar and more diffuse. I will call it the process insight. The basic idea is this: most real problems, involving as they do idiosyncratic situations and diverse people, have no solutions or right answers. The most one can hope for is to bring people together, organize a process for the resolution of the problem, and enable them to solve the problem for themselves.

This insight is pervasive in American business schools, where the case method of teaching is used. The original idea behind the case method was pedagogical. Professors had some answers, some models, some theories. Busy students in professional schools—students not particularly oriented toward theory—needed to get what was relevant from those answers, models, and theories. Cases were a way of rendering the professors' answers real to the students and thus motivating the students to learn what the professors wanted.

But a funny thing happened. Students often discovered difficulties with the application of professors' answers; professors began to see new problems in what the students and the cases taught them. Soon the case method changed. Instead of being a motivator to apply and to learn what the professor knew, it became a process for students (with the professor's help—less help as students become more adept) to generate and debate alternative solutions, with no pretense that what they eventually chose would be the right answer. The professor creates through the case method a process wherein students teach themselves.

Therapy has witnessed a similar transition. The meeting between therapist and patient was originally a device for eliciting from patients the deep background of their problems. The therapist would then make a diagnosis and tell patients the correct answer, perhaps doing the telling indirectly through further meetings. The analogy was medical, although the cure might have to be administered in a little trickier fashion.

Many therapists today, however, view the process differently. The therapist meets with patients to help them solve their own problems. The therapist seldom presumes to get the right answer and tell it to the patient. Rather, the therapist's job is to create a process for each patient's unique case to be worked through by that unique patient. Any cure is in the process.

Or consider ethnography. The anthropologist's distinctive contribution is "thick description," meaning an immersion in the details of a culture along with a constant cycling back to big questions like, "What does it mean to be a person in this culture?"[12] Ethnographic fieldwork is valuable as a process, not necessarily for its scientific results.

The anthropologist Renato Rosaldo relates this anecdote:

> On a foggy night a short number of years ago I found myself driving with a physicist along the mountainous stretch of Route 17 between Santa Cruz and San Jose . . . My companion opened by asking me, as only a physicist could, what anthropologists had discovered.
>
> "Discovered?" I asked, pretending to be puzzled. I was stalling for time. Perhaps something would come to me.
>
> "Yes, you know, something like the properties or the laws of other cultures."
>
> "Do you mean something like $E = mc^2$?"

---

12. Geertz, "Native's Point of View."

"Yes," he said.

Inspiration unexpectedly arrived and I heard myself saying, "There's one thing we know for sure. We all know a good description when we see one. We haven't discovered any laws of culture, but we do think there are classic ethnographies, really telling descriptions of other cultures."[13]

So, the process insight has many variations. Once you are enthralled by a process insight, you may apply it well beyond the classroom, the clinic, or the village. You may downplay the substance of constitutional negotiations and worry about whether the process allowed all parties to feel they were heard and honorably represented. Having talks, keeping the lines open, "wandering around" as a manager—these are always good. For a marriage or any other relationship to prosper, the key is communication—not so much what the partners say to each other, but that they talk.

With process elevated to such heights, substance may be demoted. As a master of process, you may begin to think you can be a novice of substance. Your job is to ask questions, not give answers. Indeed, you may get frustrated with so-called substantive experts. You may think they are naïve to think that any theory would be applicable to human beings and social situations in their infinite variety. You may find all talk about "objective truth" and "substantive justice" a bit unreal. Best, you say, to leave truth to a jury or a peer review, and justice to an elected parliament.

You may be pleased that others do not share this view. Curiously, you may be valued as a consultant or therapist or teacher even by those who don't have the process insight, precisely because you never say they are wrong, and you put them in the position of making the decision.

There are ways to convey the insight to others. The most effective method is to ask people to lead a class or a therapeutic session according to the insight's assumptions that they will not provide the answers but those in the session will. It often turns out to be easier to facilitate an absorbing discussion than to give an absorbing lecture. (Most students would rather talk than listen.) Particularly prone to adopt the insight are people in fields where answers are few and people in fields with answers who don't themselves happen to have them.

Academics with the process insight tend toward relativism. Methodologists study the cases and the patients and the processes and tend to conclude that it all depends on circumstances which combinations work best. This relativistic proclamation carries little practical weight, except as a reinforcement for the big aha!

---

13. Rosaldo, *Culture and Truth*, 33.

Though academic studies of the process insight yield little of prescriptive value, some practical fields are thick with the holders of this insight. Consider, for example, negotiators and aficionados of case law. When applied to economic and social policy, the insight is above all anti-theoretical. Things simply cannot be decided deductively or derived from a statistical model. It all depends and should depend on the process of getting people together to solve the problem.

The process insight can degenerate. In its emphasis on specifics, it may lose the general and theoretical—even when they might help us to understand the specifics. The insight invites charlatans and encourages vagueness: this is what happens when process and context are elevated above all. Decision-making may be left to anarchy or to the sheer exercise of personal magnetism on a group. Theory disappears and with it, rigor, science, and moral rules that cut across cases.

IMPLICATIONS

There are many other big ahas around, insights that help us make sense of a range of problems and paradoxes. It is perilous to generalize from a sample of four, and even with these four I have engaged in considerable playful simplification. But is it possible that big ahas share a pattern?

Abstract, simple, and surprising.[14] It is not, of course, that the four discussed above are not full of elaborations, tangents, and science. They go well beyond a few paragraphs' summary. But big insights are at once simple and surprising, at least once you possess them. As they resolve an apparent paradox, they suddenly take on an *obvious* quality. They generate an aha!

Wide applicability. Big insights have a number of fruitful applications within the fields from which they emerge. More importantly, they have suggestive applications beyond those fields, ranging from our personal relationships to the state of the world. They help us look at life differently.

Psychological side effects. A big insight costs something to attain and then effortlessly provides debating points that undercut those who do not have the insight. This combination has predictable and lamentable human consequences. We may become so proud of having acquired the insight that we avoid or even denigrate details, contexts, and other big insights. To those who hold a big insight, its truth and relevance is obvious. Those without the insight may be deemed naïve, ignorant, or unworthy.

---

14. "Perhaps great transforming ideas always contain only a limited number of truly provable assumptions—enough to establish some lasting roots in observation while branching out into new world-images." Erikson, "Autobiographic Notes," 751.

A process of transferal. Each insight has a somewhat costly methodology for conveying it to another. I speculate that optimally difficult transferability is a condition for a big insight to become an ideology.

The erosion of insight. What strikes me most about these insights is that each has degenerate versions. These have common features. An insight that begins as a strikingly helpful simplification and clarification of the world can become a painfully unhelpful complete view of the world. "There follow unintelligent policies and inept courses of action," writes the philosopher Bernard Lonergan. "The situation deteriorates to demand still further insights, and as they are blocked, policies become more unintelligent and more inept. What is worse, the deteriorating situation seems to provide the uncritical, biased mind with factual evidence in which the bias is claimed to be verified."[15]

KEEP MULTIPLE INSIGHTS IN MIND

Maturity of mind and sensibility allows us to inhabit the tentative, George Steiner once declared.[16] A big insight should open our eyes, not narrow our vision. The psychologist Brian Little writes, "Generally speaking, the more numerous the lenses or frames through which you can make sense of the world, the more adaptive it is. Having too few constructs or insufficiently validated ones can create problems, particularly when life is moving quickly, and you are trying to make sense of it."[17]

Note both "too few" and "insufficiently validated." The former acknowledges that theories are multiple and usefully multiple. The latter acknowledges that theories can vary in their validity.

Let us return to Thomas Kuhn's big aha! Kuhn was able to apply his insight about understanding Aristotle to understanding paradigm shifts in scientific theorizing. Transitions from one theory to the next, he said, are not captured by the conventional scientific method; they involve something like a conversion experience.

Many of his followers took this relativism to extremes. But Kuhn, I believe, was eventually able to combine *both* relativism *and* objectivity, *both* respect for different paradigms *and* respect for differences in those paradigms' success. "First, there are many ways to read a text, and the ones most accessible to a modern are often inappropriate when applied to the past. Second, that plasticity of texts does not place all ways of reading on a par,

15. Lonergan, *Insight*, Introduction.
16. Steiner, *Real Presences*, 176.
17. Little, *Me, Myself, and Us*, 4.

for some of them (ultimately, one hopes, only one) possess plausibility and coherence absent from others."[18] For Kuhn, this meant recognizing that science involves socially determined frameworks for making meaning—and yet also appreciating that science progresses by making more successful predictions that, slowly and fitfully, transcend and transform the paradigms.

BOTH/AND

In the summer after my first year of graduate school, I worked in Peru's Institute of National Planning. The revolutionary government wanted to evaluate the foreign aid it received. Over two hundred aid projects were underway. They ranged from rural roads to immunization to environmental protection to the development of the fishing industry.

The Minister of Planning explained what he was seeking. "We want to tell the donors what *we* want and need, not just take what they are giving. Last week, someone from UNIDO was here and said, 'Would you like this project? We have funding for it. But if you don't, we'll take it to Ecuador.' We need evidence to be able to say, 'This kind of project works well; this kind doesn't—and given our national plan, here's what we'd like you donors to do.' Can you help me with this?"

Fresh from courses in economics, statistics, and modeling, I imagined addressing the minister's question this way. We would begin with the country's social welfare function, basically its weighting of its many goals. In the economics I'd been learning, such functions faced daunting theoretical challenges but in principle could lay the foundation for a national plan. Using the social welfare function, you would be able to evaluate the social benefits and costs of each of the projects according to Peru's goals, and not, say, UNIDO's. Then you'd apply statistics and econometrics. I imagined an equation with each project's benefit-cost ratio on the left-hand side and, on the right-hand side the variables the minister mentioned about each project's characteristics, such as sector, donor, budget, degree of popular participation, and so forth. With that dream equation, you could estimate what kinds of projects were most socially beneficial, given Peru's objectives.

So, I told the Minister of Planning, "Can do," and went looking for the National Plan and for the evaluations of each of the two-hundred-plus projects.

The Peruvian National Plan had just been published. Over the weekend, I devoured it. Lots of lofty goals, but nothing at all about a social

18. Kuhn, *Essential Tension*, xii.

welfare function. The next week I met the Minister of Planning and asked him about the social welfare function.

"Our social welfare *what?*" he replied.

Two assistants and I examined the ministry's files on each project. There were "evaluations" but only in terms of "this happened then" or "this money went there." We found virtually no data on social benefits and costs. After a couple of weeks, I realized my dream equation to answer the minister's question was a nightmare.

And so, I wrote to Frederick Mosteller, one of the world's foremost statisticians. I described the analytical task and its impossibility, and I implicitly blamed what he and the other professors had been teaching.

He wrote back, in effect: "People can never agree in the abstract on social benefits and costs. But they can and do agree on specific examples of outrageous success and outrageous failure. Find the outrageous successes among your projects. Study them. Compare them. Share your results and learn some more."

A quick aside: Professor Mosteller's point applies more broadly. Consider the question, "What is the meaning of life?" Even if we cannot answer that question in a general way, we may be able to agree on and appreciate exemplars of meaningful lives.[19] As the philosopher Tim Mawson points out, "A life, a period or an aspect within a life, or even an individual action within a life is said to be more deeply meaningful than another and there is a notable consensus on such first-order judgments, a consensus that spans very different theories of what the meaning of life is."[20] So, find those outrageous successes. Find the heroes.

Back to Peru: we followed Professor Mosteller's advice. My Peruvian colleagues and I went from ministry to ministry, asking their leaders to name aid projects that had succeeded. (We left aside outrageous failures.) We did case studies of six of the projects. We also assembled for the first time a quantitative depiction of all the foreign aid Peru was receiving—how much, from whom, going where.

At the end of the summer, the Minister of Planning called a meeting. He invited the ministers and the donors. He asked me to facilitate. We summarized the descriptive data on Peru's aid projects. The participants had received in advance synopses of the six successful projects, which we quickly reviewed. Then I asked the participants, "Why do you think these projects succeeded?"

19. "When the topic of the meaning of life comes up, people often pose one of two questions: 'So, what is the meaning of life?' and 'What are you talking about?'" Metz, "Meaning."

20. Mawson, *God and Meanings*, 16.

One of the ministers said local participation was key. But another minister cited a project that had failed despite participation. One of the donors related his experiences in other countries with citizen participation of various kinds.

Soon they were in an animated discussion of what works where and why, and what "success" might mean. Peruvian wisdom and experience were evoked, and so was international knowledge. A few strategically posed questions got them to discuss something like the components of Peru's social welfare function. And together they worked through some of those right-hand-side variables—what kinds of projects seemed to make the most difference to which social objectives in these particular contexts. By the end of the session, their shared wisdom had catalyzed creative next steps for development assistance to Peru.

Frederick Mosteller's advice succeeded. One minister told the Minister of Planning that it was the best cabinet meeting they had ever had. Many donors were impressed. The French representative cabled home that the Peruvians had their act together and deserved more slack in deciding what projects would be funded and how the projects should be structured. After the meeting, the ministers subsequently worked better with the donors and better with each other.

Professor Mosteller's advice and the Peruvians' creativity provided me some big ahas. One was his insight that even when people can't define "success"—and they usually can't—they can agree on examples of "outrageous success." His advice to seek exemplars and discuss them pervades this book.[21]

Another was a *both/and* insight. Yes, I still appreciated the models and metaphors of economics, but I realized that no country possessed a social welfare function (and perhaps none ever would). I enjoyed and used statistics and econometrics, but I have since learned that the perfect equation is an illusion. But a big insight was that a well-structured discussion among diverse experts—the ministers and the donors—could fill out a kind of social welfare function and could qualitatively estimate a causal statistical model of what works where. These knowledgeable participants in effect filled out the dream equation—and this led not only to their owning that knowledge but then to applying it together in new ways. In chapter 8, you'll sample later work that confirms this insight: the science of choice and quantitative methods bolster, but do not replace, a process of collective, unpredictable problem solving. *Both/and.*

---

21. And, with the help of Professor Mosteller and others, the development of statistical tools to identify exceptional performers became the subject of my PhD dissertation.

MANAGING BIG INSIGHTS

Big insights are powerful and addictive. Used correctly, they reveal across many phenomena some features that we had not seen. Used incorrectly, they narrow our vision, stunt our curiosity, and fuel our arrogance. One antidote is to keep in mind both the insight and, metaphorically, its opposite. *Both/ and* is one method of avoiding the slide from insight to ideology. So is being aware of and indeed experimenting with many big insights. We benefit from being exposed to lots of big ahas and from having them close at hand as we work on our personal and social challenges.

This doesn't mean each of us has to be multidisciplinary. We may still want zealous economists, Marxists, process experts, etc. to be looking at the same issue. But we may advise that their fruitful coexistence is enhanced by (1) a forum where they can provide to an audience their different insights (and where they can hear each other) and (2) their being cognizant of alternative big insights—and of the dangers of insights becoming ideologies.

So too in our lives. We may gravitate toward one or another big insight and from there begin to feel the temptations of dogmatism. If we are aware of this tendency, we may step back and consider how other big insights might apply to the problems we are working on, including our own search for full human lives. As societies and as individuals, we face the challenge of managing big insights—assessing them, playing with them, using them without oversimplifying or overamplifying, and avoiding unwitting slides into ideology.

7

Gratitude

An insight is often perceived as a gift, as something coming from outside our will. Recognizing that fosters gratitude. The poet Gary Snyder says, "You get a good poem and you don't know where it came from. 'Did I say that?' And so all you feel is: you feel humility and you feel gratitude."[1]

And gratitude in turn engenders sharing and serving. Margaret Visser, author of *The Gift of Thanks*, puts it this way: "Being aware of goodness received makes the 'knowing' mind want to find out where more good is needed and to do it, in response. Love's insight turns, through the pivotal feeling of gratitude, into love's action."[2] The classicist and poet Lewis Hyde describes artistic insight as a gift. "I would like to speak of gratitude as a labor undertaken by the soul to effect the transformation after a gift has been received. Between the time a gift comes to us and the time we pass it along, we suffer gratitude . . . Passing the gift along is the act of gratitude that finishes the labor."[3]

As we seek the implications of our callings and our insights, gratitude is a key step. Gratitude is good for us. And, though some people seem to be innately more thankful than others, we can learn to be more grateful, in a variety of ways.

Research on gratitude[4] shows:

1. Snyder, *Real Work*, 79.
2. Visser, *Gift of Thanks*, 629.
3. Hyde, *Gift*, 60.
4. Here and elsewhere in this chapter I am indebted to Emmons, *Thanks!*

- As a personality trait, individuals vary widely in the amount of gratitude they feel and express.

- People who feel more gratitude are happier and less likely to be stressed or depressed.

- Gratitude has one of the strongest links with mental health and satisfaction with life of any personality variable. A recent study finds that "gratitude not only has direct effects on quality of life, but also has indirect effects through perceived stress and mental health."[5]

- Grateful people tend to have better social relationships and contribute more to the harmony of family and community.

And we can learn to be more grateful. One review of the scientific literature puts it this way: "Gratitude interventions lead to greater gratitude, life satisfaction, optimism, prosocial behavior, positive affect, and well-being, as well as decreased negative affect."[6] Another review of meta-analyses in psychology concludes drily that "gratitude interventions can lead to improvements for numerous outcomes, including happiness."[7]

LEARNING TO BE THANKFUL

How is gratitude learned? In English-speaking countries, we teach our children relentlessly to say "thank you." Do you remember all the time you spent prompting your preschoolers with "What do you say now?" For children in America, thanking is believed to be the very last of the social graces they acquire. Most children don't manage to produce "thank you" spontaneously until sometime between the ages of four and six. A study in England asked parents to draw up a list of the most desirable children's manners. Saying "thank you" was at the top of the list.

As a result of all this training, polite native speakers of English may say "thank you" a hundred times or more a day. One scholar estimates that thanking is performed twice as often in English than in other cultures and languages. It becomes ingrained to the point that in aphasia or Alzheimer's disease saying "thank you" is one of the last things that's forgotten. Our constant reiteration of "thank you" seems odd to many foreigners. "For speakers of Lao (Southeast Asia) or Siwu (western Africa), saying 'thank you' is so rare that it may be perceived as bizarre or out of place, whereas

5. Valikhani et al., "Gratitude and Quality of Life," 40.

6. Ritu and Anand, "Gratitude Interventions," 1232.

7. Dickens, "Meta-Analyses of Gratitude Interventions," 93.

English speakers in foreign contexts sometimes find it rude when gratitude is left unspoken."[8] In the novel *The Newlyweds*, a Bangladeshi immigrant in America thanks a cousin in Dhaka for looking after her parents. Her cousin rebukes her for sounding like a foreigner (or "bideshi" in Bangla): "You are becoming a *bideshi* over there—'thank you' this and 'thank you' that."[9] Japanese people tend to say "I'm sorry" instead of "thank you." "Please pass the soy sauce," one says. "Here you go," says the other. "I'm very sorry," says the first.

But the gratitude we consider in this chapter is deeper than custom or politeness. We feel grateful for a gift, be the gift an object or a kindness or sheer grace. Gratitude is a feeling of joy and the desire to reciprocate. Gratitude may sometimes be accompanied by a sense of indebtedness or obligation, but its essence is a feeling quite unlike anything that accompanies a payment or a contract. A disposition to gratitude helps and encourages us to carry out our responsibility in life, which is to grow in love.

The opposites of gratitude are superiority, narcissism, a sense of entitlement, and selfishness. So are thoughtlessness and forgetfulness. In *The Devil's Dictionary*, Ambrose Bierce defined "ingratitude" as "a form of self-respect that is not inconsistent with acceptance of favors." (A great book, by the way. Do you know how Bierce defined "saint"? "A dead sinner revised and edited.")

How do we develop a deeper gratitude beyond saying thanks on cue? Research shows that these two practices engender gratitude:

- Keep a gratitude journal for recording the reasons, events, and help received that merit your gratitude, in the past and present and as they occur in the future. A number of studies have randomly assigned subjects to keep three kinds of journals. One group records specific things they are thankful for. Another group records things that have bothered them that day. And a third group receives the neutral instruction to write down some of the things that happened that day.

  The results: the grateful group is happier, more successful in fulfilling their goals, exercises more, and reports better relationships with others.

- A second idea is to write a gratitude letter. The psychologist Martin Seligman developed this intervention, which he now uses in class as well. You think of someone to whom you are grateful but whom you have never properly thanked. You compose a three-hundred-word testimonial to that person. And then you deliver it in person, not telling

8. Floyd et al., "Universals and Cultural Diversity," 8.
9. Freudenberger, *Newlyweds*.

the purpose, just saying, "I want to come over and see you." The results are emotional, and then measurable in the gratitude and attitude of both people even months later.[10]

FROM ATTITUDE TO BEHAVIOR, OR VICE VERSA?

What is the essence of these techniques? Let me ask you a question. Does behavior tend to follow attitudes or do attitudes tend to follow behavior?

William James, writing more than a hundred years ago, argued that changing behavior leads to changes in attitudes, not the other way around. He shared this finding in one of his "lectures to teachers."

> There is, accordingly, no better known or more generally useful precept in the moral training of youth, or in one's personal self-discipline, than that which bids us pay primary attention to what we do and express, and not to care too much for what we feel . . .
>
> Thus the sovereign voluntary path to cheerfulness, if our spontaneous cheerfulness be lost, is to sit up cheerfully, to look round cheerfully, and to act and speak as if cheerfulness were already there. If such conduct does not make you soon feel cheerful, nothing else on that occasion can. So to feel brave, act as if we *were* brave, use all our will to that end, and a courage-fit will very likely replace the fit of fear. Again, in order to feel kindly toward a person to whom we have been inimical, the only way is more or less deliberately to smile, to make sympathetic inquiries, and to force ourselves to say genial things. One hearty laugh together will bring enemies into a closer communion of heart than hours spent on both sides in inward wrestling with the mental demon of uncharitable feeling. To wrestle with a bad feeling only pins our attention on it, and keeps it still fastened in the mind: whereas, if we act as if from some better feeling, the old bad feeling soon folds its tent . . . and silently steals away.[11]

One day years ago, our seven-year-old daughter Kristen came into the study and asked, "Daddy, what are you reading?" It happened to be this essay by William James, and I shared parts of it with her. She liked it. A few weeks later, she came to me again and told me about a project for her second-grade class. Each student was to choose a famous American, dress up like him or her, and, in a special class with parents present, talk about his or her life.

10. Seligman, *Authentic Happiness.*
11. James, "Gospel of Relaxation."

"How about if I am William James?"

A week later, there we were in class. She had on a beard and a top hat. She said a sentence about who James was, and then in her own words summarized the idea that if we change our behavior, we change our attitudes. (Her mother and I felt very grateful.)

Act grateful, express gratitude, and we will soon feel grateful. Accepting a true gift can itself be a grateful act; gratitude is virtue in the receiver.

FROM AWARENESS TO THANKFULNESS

A key to this virtue is simply being *aware*. In the epilogue to her autobiographical book *An American Childhood*, Annie Dillard ponders what she as a middle-aged author has in common with the girl and adolescent she has just written about.

> Where have they gone, those other dim dots that were you: you in the flesh swimming in a swift river, swinging a bat on the first pitch, opening a footlocker with a screwdriver, inking and painting clowns on celluloid, stepping out of a revolving door into the swift crowd on a sidewalk, being kissed and kissing till your brain grew smooth, stepping out of the cold woods into a warm field full of crows, or lying awake in a bed aware of your legs and suddenly aware of all of it, that the ceiling above you was under the sky—in what country, what town?
>
> You may wonder, that is, as I sometimes wonder privately, but it doesn't matter. For it is not you or I that is important, neither what sort we might be nor how we came to be each where we are. What is important is anyone's coming awake and discovering a place, finding in full orbit a spinning globe one can lean over, catch, and jump on. What is important is the moment of opening a life and feeling it touch—with an electric hiss and cry—this speckled mineral sphere, our present home.[12]

Here is how she concludes the book: "I am here now, with this my own dear family, up here at this high latitude, out here at the farthest exploratory tip of this my present bewildering age. And still I break up through the skin of awareness a thousand times a day, as dolphins burst through the seas, and dive again, and rise, and dive."[13]

Deeply felt gratitude is a species of awe. It implies a sense of one's tininess before the wonder of the universe, of the earth and all of nature, of one's

---

12. Dillard, *American Childhood*, 248–49.
13. Dillard, *American Childhood*, 258.

unique self "breaking up through the skin of awareness." Awe, like gratitude, is the opposite of what we call "taking things for granted."

In 1795, the young Scottish physician and naturalist Mungo Park set off to explore West Africa.[14] Tall, sandy-haired, and quiet, Park was barely twenty-four; he had already traveled to Sumatra. Now his goal was to be the first European to reach the Niger River and the legendary cities of Timbuktu and Haussa. He traveled up the Gambia River two hundred miles to an outpost called Pisania, which had three white people, where he spent seven months learning one of the local languages and recovering from malaria. Eventually, he and two bearers headed east. He had many adventures, including four months' captivity under a Moorish chief. He escaped and eventually reached the Niger River. He went down the river as far as Silla, where, exhausted, he decided to turn back short of Timbuktu.

On the return journey he was robbed and stripped by Moorish bandits. They took everything—his horse, his compass, his hat, all his clothes except his trousers and his battered boots. They had evidently intended to kill him but saw him as a feeble white man beneath contempt. They did throw his hat back to him—not realizing that it contained the papers of his travel journal folded up in the band.

"After they were gone, I sat for some time looking round me with amazement and terror . . . I saw myself in a vast wilderness in the depth of the rainy season, naked and alone; surrounded by savage animals, and men still more savage. I was 500 miles from the nearest European settlement. All these circumstances crowded at once on my recollection; and I confess my spirits began to fail me. I considered my fate as certain, and that I had no alternative but to lie down and perish."[15]

But then something curious happened. As he hung his head in exhaustion and misery, Mungo Park's gaze wandered over the bare ground at his feet. He noticed a tiny piece of flowering moss pushing up through the stony earth beside his boot. His scientific interest was sparked, and, leaning forward to examine the minute plant, for one moment he forgot his terrible situation. He carefully described this movement out of paralyzing despair:

> At this moment, painful as my reflections were, the extraordinary beauty of a small moss in fructification, irresistibly caught my eye. I mention this to show from what trifling circumstances the mind will sometimes derive consolation; for though the whole plant was not larger than the top of one of my fingers,

14. The story of Mungo Park is drawn from Holmes, *Age of Wonder*.
15. Park, *Life and Travels*, 94.

I could not contemplate the delicate conformation of its roots, leaves, and capsula, without admiration.

In that moment of wonder, Park was transformed.

Can the Being (thought I) who planted, watered, and brought to perfection, in this obscure part of the world, a thing which seems of so small importance, look with unconcern upon the situation and suffering of creatures formed after his own image?—surely not! Reflections like these would not allow me to despair. I started up, and disregarding both hunger and fatigue, traveled forwards, assured that relief was at hand; and I was not disappointed.[16]

He soon fell in with two friendly shepherds and continued westward toward the sea. Miraculously, he found he could pay his passage by writing phrases from the Koran on loose scraps of paper, saved from his journal, and selling these as religious charms.

He finally reached Pisania on June 10, 1797, and then Scotland on December 22. He was greeted with delight and astonishment, for people had assumed him dead. Two years later, his book *Travels in the Interior of Africa* was published, and it became a classic.

Mungo Park's awe kindled gratitude and, in turn, gave him the resolution to continue. To encourage gratitude, we should develop what G. K. Chesterton called "the ancient instinct of astonishment," the surprise and wonder that quickly turn into gratitude. "There is no way in which a man [or a woman] can earn a star or deserve a sunset."[17]

And so, in these many ways, we can learn to be—and resolve to be—more grateful. Today, tomorrow, and in the days that follow, may we, like Mungo Park but without the malaria or the robbers, be aware beneath our feet of the wonders of creation. At night, may we, like Annie Dillard, be aware of our legs under the sheets, and imagine the starry skies above.

And may we continually remind ourselves that the gifts we most appreciate—"the gift we long for, the gift that, when it comes, speaks commandingly to the soul and irresistibly moves us"[18]—should kindle our desire to share and serve.

16. Park, *Life and Travels*, 95

17. Chesterton, *Francis of Assisi*, 80.

18. Hyde, *Gift*, xxiii.

8

Share and Serve

Heroes in legend and literature, in history and all around us, are characterized by sharing their callings and insights, by serving without obligation or self-regard. We know this, and yet *sharing* and *serving* have two immediate disadvantages. They don't sound like much fun. And, more subtly, they both seem upon reflection to have limits. Both disadvantages raise questions, not so much about whether to share and serve, but about how much to do so.

And then comes the question of how.

NOT FUN

The word "sharing" may evoke negative memories. As a child, when you were told to share your toys, didn't it really mean fewer toys for you? Didn't "sharing time" in elementary school really mean boring stories about stamp collections and summer vacations? And now, in a political or economic discussion, when people talk about "sharing" does it seem like a code word for taxation, redistribution, or confiscation?

"Serving" doesn't fare much better. It slides into words and meanings we don't naturally like, like "servant." One of August Strindberg's autobiographical works shocked his contemporaries from the title on—he called it *Son of a Servant*. The heartiest rebuke I ever heard from my English-born grandmother was when she once scolded us children for the way she thought we were acting toward her daughter. "You treat your moth-uh like a suh-vent," she sputtered. Her uncharacteristically hostile tone sent us the message that to be a servant is low indeed.

Serving may suggest "servility." One dictionary's definition is "slavish, truckling obedience." Sound attractive?

Even the word "service" has its unpleasantries. Stallions are said to "service" mares, and that usage carries over to low renditions of human sexual intercourse. In Spanish, a toilet is a *servicio*.

If a Gallup Poll were to ask people, "What are your favorite things to do?" almost nobody would unreflectively respond with "sharing and serving."

LIMITS

As a junior in college, I watched an economics professor prove mathematically that there is an optimal amount of altruism. Complete altruism is inefficient, he demonstrated. It doesn't make sense, for example, for you to walk all the way across a room to open a door for someone only a pace away from the door—someone equally able and strong. It's nice, but it's inefficient. We should, the professor said, economize on altruism. Sharing and serving have optimal limits.

At least he didn't suggest that altruism should be set at zero. Sometimes elementary microeconomics is interpreted that way. Long ago, Bernard de Mandeville argued that the best outcome for society would generally be reached if each person simply follows his or her own interests.[1] Private selfishness, even some amounts of vice, would lead to social optimality. Moreover, people's attempts to help others, through things like sharing, might well backfire in the aggregate.

Some economists have argued that the shortcomings of communist and of populist economic policies—both of which seem to be altruistically redistributing resources to workers and peasants and ordinary people—result from trying to share too much and in ineffective ways. Efficiency, a god of economics, seems to limit sharing and serving. (Noting these points does not signify agreement with them.[2])

Other economists have shown how institutions replace sharing. Many examples of sharing in premodern societies are analyzed as ways to pool risks or encourage trade or enforce contracts or define property rights. As the ability to measure things and communicate information develop, formal institutions arise that take over more and more of the functions of

1. Mandeville, *Fable of the Bees.*

2. Indeed, the proper rebuttal is Sandel, "Market Reasoning."

traditional sharing.[3] One implication is that economic and political development renders many traditional forms of sharing obsolete. Sharing will
diminish over time.

Beyond economics, do some modern intellectuals at least unconscious-
ly seek ways to avoid and undermine sharing? The sociologist John Murray
Cuddihy thought so. He contended that a common problem for emerging
European intellectuals from Marx to Freud to Lévi-Strauss was how to avoid
"the ritual exchange of gifts we call 'civility.'"[4] Roughly, "civility" meant to
share and serve without a market or a rule or an order from the state. Civility discomfited some of these often socially awkward, theoretically gifted
intellectuals. Cuddihy argued that vastly different intellectual contributions
from Freudian psychology to modern socialism (and sociology) had as a
unifying motif a desire to avoid being criticized for personal shortcomings
in civility. (Again, noting these points does not imply agreeing with them.)

THE WAYS WE SHARE

How much we should share is one question. *How* we should share is another.

In his Depression-era novel *Heaven's My Destination*, Thornton Wilder
describes a young man full of religion who eagerly launches forth to share
his insight with the world.[5] On a train, George Marvin Brush sits next
to an old man. The two begin to talk. Immediately, the old man lays on
an intense fundamentalist pitch. He gives George no chance to speak. The
older man has an insight and, by God, he is going to share it. George can't
even say, "I know, I know—I'm saved just like you!" He has no choice but to
withstand the onslaught, and through his ordeal he may reckon that the old
man's method is not successful. Reciting a formula, even God's formula, is
usually not effective sharing and serving.

An Example from International Development

Let me give an example from my own field, international development. The
poorest countries are often ill-formed nations, residues of a colonial world
where they were washed over with constitutions and freedoms and educa-
tions that only patchily took hold. These nations evince extreme versions of
phenomena we recognize in the so-called developed world. Why do "free

3. Posner, "Primitive Society."
4. Cuddihy, *Ordeal of Civility*, 3.
5. Wilder, *Heaven's My Destination*, 92–95.

markets" so often disadvantage the poor, and what might be done to make markets work better and more fairly? How can corruption be reduced, if never eliminated? What can be done about self-reproducing, self-protecting élites? What can be done to reduce racial and ethnic inequalities?[6]

It has been my privilege to work on these issues with people all over the world. My calling has been not just to write books but to help local people share their own and other people's knowledge, and to share whatever quasi-scientific insights I and others might provide, in ways that stimulate locals to think more creatively and act more constructively. We begin with the audience: what do they need? And then we ask, what and how can we share?

Let's contrast two approaches. One is that of the expert. The scientist, the doctor, the therapist, the teacher knows what works. How? Ideally, from validated theory and empirical evidence about your situation. The expert's job is to appraise you, apply the theory, and prescribe your treatment: what should happen to you (what medicine, fertilizer, therapy . . .) and what you should do (exercises, readings, prohibitions . . .). Your job as patient or student or country is to comply.

Needless to say, many people do not enjoy being told what to do—nor do sovereign nations like being told what steps they must take to receive international aid. In policy advising, the expert model is severely strained.[7]

In contrast, a second approach says that both outsiders and insiders have expertise, and the task is to combine forces. Locals have tacit and explicit knowledge about local settings. But they may lack access to some of the best data and techniques of data collection to calibrate their challenges. They may not be familiar with examples of what has worked elsewhere. They may benefit from exposure to models and theories that can be used to suggest frameworks for action. The challenge becomes how to bring what they know best (local contexts and possibilities) with what outside experts may offer (facts, examples, frameworks).

Here is a method called "convening" that has proved useful in many settings:

1. "We have a problem here." First, share *data* about the challenge being confronted—data from the local setting and data from outside that help locals contextualize their situation.

2. "It can be done." Next comes a *success story*—a hero of development, if you will. Let's look together at an example where this problem has

---

6. Klitgaard, *Adjusting to Reality.*

7. Easterly, *Tyranny of Experts.*

been tackled more or less successfully. What were the transformative decisions they made? How did they make those choices real?

3. "Here's how." Then comes sharing a *model* or framework or theory that helps people rethink their alternatives.

How these things are shared can make all the difference. In convenings, participants consider the data together, work through the success story in a problem-solving mode, and analyze the model or framework before addressing their own situations. And when they finally do examine their own problems, the outside expert's role is indirect. "Let's look again at the framework or model. Let's apply the same analytical and practical spirit of analyzing various alternatives, which we used in the case study of that success story." At the end, the expert does not prescribe; he or she humbly asks, "How can I help you?"[8]

An Example of Convening[9]

In June 2010, Benigno Aquino III was elected president of the Philippines. As did his campaign, his inaugural address focused on fighting corruption:

> During the campaign we said, "If no one is corrupt, no one will be poor." That is no mere slogan for posters—it is the defining principle that will serve as the foundation of our administration.
> Our foremost duty is to lift the nation from poverty through honest and effective governance . . . No more influence-peddling, no more patronage politics, no more stealing. No more sirens, no more short cuts, no more bribes.[10]

When Aquino took office, the Philippines did not fare well on various measures of corruption and competitiveness. Transparency International's Corruption Perceptions Index 2010 ranked the Philippines 133rd out of 178 countries, tied with such countries as Bangladesh, Honduras, and Zimbabwe. In the 2009–10 Global Competitiveness Index, the Philippines ranked 87th out of 132 countries, trailing such countries as Guatemala and the Gambia. In 2010, the International Finance Corporation ranked the Philippines 144th of 183 countries in terms of "ease of doing business."

8. For more on this method, see Klitgaard, *Culture and Development Manifesto*, especially chapter 10.

9. The following is based on Klitgaard, "Engaging Corruption."

10. "Inaugural Address."

The Philippines was cruelly called "the cripple of Asia," poorer than its high-flying neighbors, growing more slowly, and more corrupt.

Several weeks after Aquino took office, there was an all-day convening in Malacañang Palace. The participants were the new cabinet secretaries, as well as the heads of the Central Bank, the Customs Bureau, and the Bureau of Internal Revenue. Their goal was to catalyze the first steps of a practical strategy to fight corruption. They went through the steps of a convening:

1. *Data* were discussed about the extent and social costs of various kinds of corruption in the Philippines compared with other countries.

2. *Success story.* Then, in a two-part case study, the participants analyzed a country that had successfully reduced corruption.

3. *Model.* Next, they worked through economic models of corruption, leading to a one-page framework for policy analysis.

Thus stimulated, they turned to their own country. The problems of corruption are complex; the Philippines' setting is unique. And yet the data, the case study, and the economic models became, with these participants in this process, a catalyst for creative problem solving. By eight o'clock that evening they had devised an outline of a national strategy, which three of the cabinet secretaries elaborated on Sunday and Monday and briefed to the president on Tuesday.

As President Aquino's intrepid anti-corruption campaign developed, it included identifying and punishing some major offenders, forging new partnerships with business and civil society to analyze corrupt systems and improve accountability, using citizen scorecards to gauge the performance of government agencies, implementing radical reforms in bottom-up budgeting and evaluation, enhancing coordination across key government agencies, and more. International donors and lenders played key roles in supporting many of these initiatives.

The results were remarkable. In September 2014, the World Economic Forum called the Philippines the "most improved country overall" in terms of global competitiveness over the previous four years. Citizens' satisfaction with the government and President Aquino's popularity were unprecedented compared with previous Filipino presidents at similar times in their terms of office. And there were many economic benefits. Investment rose from 16.6 percent of GDP in 2009 to 22.5 percent in 2016. Foreign direct investment grew fivefold in five years and reached an all-time high of $10 billion in 2017. Unemployment hit a record low of 5.7 percent, and inflation dropped to 1.6 percent.

Finally, growth in GDP averaged 6.5 percent from 2015 to 2017, eclipsing most of the Asian Tigers. The cripple of Asia no more.

The Philippines still had a long way to go, but progress in the Philippines under President Aquino was tangible. Even in a country plagued by systemic corruption, improvement was possible, with significant developmental benefits.

This convening approach to sharing is useful for problems that have these attributes:

- A decision that is transformative in the senses we have already discussed: a country faces long-term choices for a highly uncertain future, and those choices must somehow take account of future generations whose values and priorities are in some sense unknowable.

- A problem whose solution, or even whose identification, seems to require creativity and energy, not just an understanding of well-known theorems or recipes.

- An opportunity for people who ordinarily don't talk or work well together to consider new ways of tackling an issue.

- A chance to learn from data and case studies, with the goal not of copying but of being intrigued and inspired. "I never would have thought of that." "Interesting how they began over there rather than over here."

- And, at the risk of misunderstanding, a situation that allows the possibility for a humble sort of conversion experience, in the sense that some people may come to see their priorities and their choices in an entirely different light. "Aha! I never thought of corruption as a crime of calculation." Or even as simple as, "We can do something about corruption, instead of just accepting it as the way life is."

Applying This Method to Our Transformative Decisions

We can apply similar ideas to helping ourselves with our own development challenges. When they make transformative decisions about their strategies, countries must try to imagine what the world will be like many years into the future, as well as what their people will be like.[11] So too must we, when we

---

11. Transformative choices face all countries. Consider investments in "infrastructure" such as roads, bridges, ports, and energy grids. A key question is, as the title of a 2021 workshop sponsored by the U.S. National Academy of Sciences put it, "How Do We Build Infrastructure for a Future We Can't See?"

face our own transformative decisions—where to move, what career to try, whether or when to have a family. We can have a little convening of our own:

1. *Data.* Locating ourselves with data has several benefits. We realize with relief that we're not alone. We can assess how we are faring by comparing ourselves with others. What upheavals have happened or threaten us? What are our options? Let's collect information about them, comparing ourselves and our situations with other people's.

2. *Success story.* Identify heroes who, facing upheavals and decisions like ours, have succeeded—not reaching perfection, but moving along a dynamic path of improvement. Explore their stories. If we know of real-life heroes of relevance, perhaps we even ask them to discuss things with us.

   The head of a successful program to help runaway girls in San Francisco explained the key ideas. To paraphrase: "The first thing is to show them they're not alone. This is often such a relief for them. We help them with their basic needs, like shelter and food. And then we have them meet some former runaways who have succeeded. They've made it off the streets and into school or jobs. The older girls tell their stories, and the younger girls are motivated to move ahead."

3. *Model.* Then we can apply to our situation the steps of calling, insight, gratitude, and sharing and serving.

   a. Work our way through our calling and possible alternatives, perhaps including some as large as those in chapter 5.

   b. Recall our discussion of big insights in chapter 6, and try to re-capture or reconsider our own big insights.

   c. Ask how we can be grateful, even now, for small things and large ones in our lives.

   d. Consider, as we have in this chapter, how we might share and serve with compassion.

Appendix 2 provides a more detailed checklist to stimulate our self-assessment and guide our tentative progress down our own paths to prevailing.

RECEIVING AND GIVING

As we share and serve, we have to beware of casting ourselves as the experts, the superiors, the generous ones. Pope Francis has warned against proselytizing.[12] His namesake, St. Francis of Assisi, is often (but contro-versially) cited as having said, "Preach the gospel at all times. Use words if necessary."[13] Move forward with deeds.

We should also be wary of being The Teacher. "The true knight of faith," Kierkegaard admonished, "is a witness, never a teacher, and therein lies his deep humanity, which is worth a great deal more than this silly participation in others' weal and woe which is honored by the name of sympathy, whereas in fact it is nothing but vanity."[14]

And we should even be suspicious of giving, especially of character-izing ourselves as *givers* and others as *takers*. John Steinbeck wrote a re-markable essay about his friend Ed Ricketts, the unorthodox scientist and local legend who was the model for the character of Doc in *Cannery Row*. After Ed's death, Steinbeck tried to analyze "the great talent that was in Ed Ricketts, that made him so loved and needed and makes him so missed now that he is dead." Steinbeck eventually decided that Ed's talent lay in

> his ability to receive, to receive anything from anyone, to receive gratefully and thankfully and make the gift seem very fine. Be-cause of this everyone felt good in giving to Ed—a present, a thought, anything.
>
> Perhaps the most overrated virtue on our list of shoddy virtues is that of giving. Giving builds up the ego of the giver, makes him superior and higher and larger than the receiver. Nearly always, giving is a selfish pleasure, and in many cases it is downright destructive and evil thing. One has only to remem-ber some of our wolfish financiers who spend two-thirds of their lives clawing fortunes out of the guts of society and the latter third pushing it back. It is not enough to suppose that their phi-lanthropy is a kind of frightened restitution, or that their natures change when they have enough. Such a nature never has enough and natures do not change that readily. I think the impulse is the same in both cases. For giving can bring the same sense of superiority as getting does, and philanthropy may be another kind of spiritual avarice.

---

12. *Pope Francis.*

13. No record exists of St. Francis saying exactly that, and in his times his sermons were revered. But he did say, "It is no use walking anywhere to preach unless our walk-ing is our preaching" and "As for me, I desire this privilege from the Lord, that never may I have any privilege from man, except to do reverence to all, and to convert the world by obedience to the Holy Rule rather by example than by word." Arpin-Ricci, "Preach the Gospel."

14. Kierkegaard, *Fear and Trembling*, 90.

It is so easy to give, so exquisitely rewarding. Receiving, on the other hand, if it be well done, requires a fine balance of self-knowledge and kindness. It requires humility and tact and great understanding of relationships. In receiving you cannot appear, even to yourself, better or stronger or wiser than the giver, although you must be wiser to do it well.[15]

Gifts can be glorious, but sometimes gifts degenerate into self-interested transactions. The sociologist Marcel Mauss wrote that gifts and sharing are "in theory voluntary, disinterested and spontaneous, but are in fact obligatory and interested. The form usually taken is that of the gift generously offered, but the accompanying behavior is formal pretense and social deception, while the transaction itself is based on obligation and economic self-interest."[16]

"It is the law of the gift," wrote H. Newell Wardle in 1931, "that it may not be summarily refused without giving offense, and a counter gift must be tendered in due season. The Maori of New Zealand class with theft failure to offer the return gift. Neglect to offer or refusal to take a gift is a declaration of war among Dyak tribes of Borneo. The Northwest Coast tribes acknowledge the potlatch to be 'fighting with favors' in place of 'war by deeds.'"[17] Wardle went on to supply many other examples and concluded by noting, "Striving for prestige and the feeling of the need of reciprocity are not absent in gift giving in modern societies."

In these functionalist narratives, gifts are bribes in disguise.

Can be. Shouldn't be.

Look at the differences between a true gift and a bribe. A bribe has a purpose: to move the recipient to serve the briber's interests. The more impersonal the medium, the better. The bribe must be delivered secretively; the recipient is usually ruined if the bribe becomes known. The bribe is exchanged for a service, and this equivalence means that the size of the bribe is important. It is intended to create an obligation. A bribe is an act of self-interest.

A gift differs from a bribe along all these dimensions. A gift is a token of affection. Its context is a personal relationship, and its intent is to convey a personal feeling. A gift is the more suitable the more it expresses the recipient's interests and the giver's tastes. Secrecy is not essential, though a gift

15. Steinbeck, *Sea of Cortez*, lxiv–lxv. Note a parallel comment by Søren Kierkegaard: "He had not even comprehended the little mystery, that it is better to give than to receive, and has no inkling of the great one, that it is far more difficult to receive than to give." Kierkegaard, *Fear and Trembling*, 113.

16. Mauss, *Gift*, 1.

17. Wardle, "Gifts and Display," 658.

may be a secret; in general, the recipient is glad to acknowledge the giver. The size of the gift is unimportant. What matters is how the donor expresses identification with the recipient, for this identification is what a gift declares. The gift is wholly the recipient's and, in the limit, creates no obligation.

In the ideal case, writes John T. Noonan Jr., a gift conveys love.

> The donee's thanks are but the ghost of a reciprocal bond. That the gift should operate coercively is indeed repugnant and painful to the donor, destructive of the liberality that is intended. Freely given, the gift leaves the donee free. When the love the gift conveys is total, donor and donee are one, so the donor has no one to whom to respond. Every gift tries to approximate this ideal case. A present of any amount is a gift when it conveys love.[18]

Noonan could have been describing sharing and serving in the heroic model. To be done well, sharing and serving must be attentive to situation, norms, and conventions. Sharing and serving have to be tailored to individuals as well—to a person's feelings, fears, and aspirations. We have received gifts of calling and insight, perhaps by someone sharing and serving us, perhaps also from heroic examples. In some sense, we owe for these gifts but only in a highly metaphorical fashion. When we say we are "indebted," we mean we are grateful; and we in turn present our sharing and serving not as a payback but as an act of love.

18. Noonan, *Bribes*, 695.

PART III

Heroes Close to Home

9

Romance and Intimacy

My research for this book was brusquely interrupted by romance. Conceptually, that is.

The precipitant was an essay by Becca Rothfeld about the collected letters of Iris Murdoch. Murdoch was a philosopher at Oxford who strayed, and flourished, as a novelist. "Her scholarly area was ethics, and her primary preoccupation was love, both romantic and platonic," Rothfeld writes. "This was a topic whose manifest importance she felt was chronically neglected by her peers, most of them analytic philosophers."[1]

Murdoch and Rothfeld are right, I thought. Romance and sex received little attention in the history of Western philosophy, and what it did receive was not good. Socrates' guy friends, lolling around the symposium, concluded that the highest physical side of romantic love was men and boys. But better to leave the sex part behind, said Socrates, and go for the ideal of beauty. Thus "Platonic love." Aristotle barely mentioned the sexual side of love, and Christian philosophers condemned it.

Dante chastely chased his beloved Beatrice into paradise. Sex and romance were not admired in the philosophy of, say, Immanuel Kant. One philosopher said Kant represented "a lifelong celibate philosopher and a stark condemnation of most sexual activity." Kant said, for example, that all non-procreative sex is to be considered worse than suicide.[2] Didn't some-

---

1. Rothfeld, "Affliction and Salvation."

2. He did say: "Love is a matter of feeling, not of willing, and I cannot love because I will to, still less because I ought to (I cannot be constrained to love); so a duty to love is an absurdity." Kant, *Metaphysics of Morals*, 161.

one once say it's impossible even to imagine a Mrs. Plato, a Mrs. Kant, a Mrs. Nietzsche?

Ah, Nietzsche. It is said that he was once smitten, that he so informed the young lady most awkwardly, then proposed marriage to her in a letter delivered through a friend who also liked her—a letter she never answered, perhaps never received (soon she had started living with the friend).[3] Is that why in *The Gay Science* Nietzsche says that women always put on an act, men must dominate, and romantic love is just an illusion, "the most ingenuous expression of egoism," a manifestation of that acting and that pretense of dominating?[4]

And so, I grabbed some of Murdoch's work, and I sent an email of praise to Rothfeld. She turned out to be finishing her first year as a graduate student in philosophy at Harvard. What, so young and already so wise?[5]

Later I was visiting Harvard and invited Rothfeld to have breakfast. I asked her how she thought philosophy should incorporate romantic love. She said—please forgive me, Ms. Rothfeld, for this summary that reflects my ignorance more than your answer—"I don't know."

I didn't either. But clearly Murdoch and Rothfeld are right. Romantic love is part of the ideal of a full human life for many people. Including me. And yet, I had left it out of my research entirely.

As we have seen, Thomas à Kempis is the foil for a view of a flourishing life that, well, avoids being fully human. His book *The Imitation of Christ* said to despise the world out there; it is a threat to your life in Christ. He didn't mention romance and intimacy, but he did warn against women. "If I were you boys, I wouldn't talk or even think about women. It ain't good for your health."

Actually, that's not Thomas à Kempis speaking. It's Howard, the saintly old prospector in the 1948 film *The Treasure of the Sierra Madre*. But Thomas would concur.

In contrast to this avoidance of the world, the extreme addict is voracious and insatiable—but eventually unsatisfied, as Joris-Karl Huysman's novel *Against Nature* memorably describes (see Box 5).

---

3. Brinton, *Nietzsche*, 55–56.

4. Nietzsche, *Gay Science*, §14, §363.

5. Which may recall a line by the great physicist Wolfgang Pauli—who at age 22 wrote a 237-page monograph on quantum mechanics that is still used today—concerning a youthful candidate for a faculty position: "So young and he has already contributed so little?" Segrè, *Faust in Copenhagen*, 268,

BOX 5. THE PALLING OF SEX ADDICTION

"A single passion, woman, might have curbed his contempt, but that, too, had palled on him. He had taken to carnal repasts with the eagerness of a crotchety man affected with a depraved appetite and given to sudden hungers, whose taste is quickly dulled and surfeited. Associating with country squires, he had taken part in their lavish suppers where, at dessert, tipsy women would unfasten their clothing and strike their heads against the tables; he had haunted the green rooms, loved actresses and singers, endured, in addition to the natural stupidity he had come to expect of women, the maddening vanity of female strolling players. Finally, satiated and weary of this monotonous extravagance and the sameness of their caresses, he had plunged into the foul depths, hoping by the contrast of squalid misery to revive his desires and stimulate his deadened senses.

"Whatever he attempted proved vain; an unconquerable ennui oppressed him."[6]

It is controversial among scientists whether a person can have an addiction to sex and romantic conquest.[7] Whatever: in my exaggeration, the addict ends up alone. It is not the solitude of the extreme ascetic but, as we saw, both of them may experience a kind of living death.

We have been investigating a different ideal type, a hero found in many traditions around the world in many forms and legends, and also in real life. We have been considering this pattern:

- The hero receives a calling.
- The hero discovers or is sent an insight that is specific to him or her and also resonates with the challenges of many.
- The hero feels grateful, as if the calling and insight were gifts.
- And the hero responds by sharing and serving, not remaining in a cell or in a castle but foraying into the real world.

The hero is an archetype of a flourishing life.

6. Huysmans, *Against the Grain*, 11.

7. Sinnott-Armstrong and Pickard, "What Is Addiction?," 860. But consider Phillips et al., "Sex Addiction."

And now, prodded by Becca Rothfeld and Iris Murdoch, I venture to consider how romantic love and intimacy might fit.

First, a reminder. In this endeavor, we're not describing neurological states; not statistically charting how many of what kinds have how much; and not calculating cultural, socioeconomic, or historical correlations. We do not aspire to necessary or sufficient conditions for a flourishing life. We've been working schematically, impressionistically. "Consider a kind of hero who . . . And even though you and I are not heroes, let's see what we might learn."

And then, an acknowledgement of awkwardness. Romantic love is entwined with sex, a subject notoriously difficult to approach deftly. Some of us have more trouble with the subject than others. The anthropologist Raymonde Carroll wrote that Americans can't stand it when French friends go on and on about their sexual conquests (and the French can't abide the American tendency to blab about money).[8] But—French, Americans, whoever nowadays—even if we feel uncomfortable, we can't seem to get away from romance and sex. They are everywhere.

LOVE LIFE LOW AND HIGH

For example, while browsing the anything-but-sexy website TechCrunch. com, I came across a news story with this opening paragraph: "Let's admit it, you probably aren't reading that romance novel for the plot. Or its literary value. Audible knows this and is today launching a new collection of romance-themed audiobooks that come with a handy feature that lets you skip right to the action. Called 'Take Me to the Good Part,' the feature will fast-forward you to the steamy section."[9]

Ah, those steamy sections. But they're not just in trash novels. Audible might consider adding Giovanni Boccaccio's *The Decameron*, written around 1350. Joan Acocella calls *The Decameron* "probably the dirtiest great book in the Western canon."[10]

Like romance novels today, *The Decameron* was written for "gracious ladies" and "amiable ladies" fascinated by the passions of love. "I offered this effort of mine," says the narrator at the end, "to ladies living in idleness rather than to anyone else . . . to dispel the melancholy with which ladies are afflicted."[11]

In *The Decameron* ten friends go wandering in the Florentine countryside. Each day for ten days, each one tells a story to the rest about an

8. Carroll, *Cultural Misunderstandings*.

9. Perez, "Audible's New Romance."

10. Acocella, "Renaissance Man."

11. Boccaccio, *Decameron*, 858.

assigned topic, such as cleverness or generosity. The resulting one hundred tales cover over eight hundred pages.

Most of the stories include saucy accounts of sexual encounters, using euphemisms like "beating the fur," "delightedly making the nightingale sing over and over again," and "since they had only traveled six miles that night, they went two more before they finally got out of bed." One unfaithful wife spent her first night with "a handsome, lusty young man" teaching him "how to sing a good half-dozen of her husband's hymns."

One of the longer stories is the saga of Alatiel, a woman so beautiful that she cannot escape the passions she inflames over a series of husbands and lovers, some of whom kill each other for her. There is a happy-ever-after when, finally, she becomes the wife of the king of Algarve. "Although she had slept with eight men perhaps ten thousand times, she not only came to the King's bed as if she were a virgin, but made him believe she really was one, and for a good many years after that, lived a perfectly happy life with him as his Queen."[12]

The Decameron's narrator reports that as they were hearing this tale, "the ladies sighed repeatedly over the lovely lady's various misadventures, but who knows what may have moved them to do so? Perhaps some of them sighed as much out of a desire for such frequent marriages as out of pity for Alatiel."[13]

In another story, a lovely, "lofty" lady overflows with passion. She is not punished for cheating on her husband because, she has the husband admit before the judge and audience, she never ever turned him down for sex, as many times as he wanted. Then she asks the judge and audience, "If he's always obtained what he needed from me and was pleased with it, what was I supposed to do—in fact, what am I supposed to do now—with the leftovers. Should I throw them to the dogs? Isn't it much better to serve some of them up to a gentleman who loves me more than his very own life than to let them go to waste or have them spoil?"[14]

It's a story of true love—but yes, it's her allusion to steamy leftovers that makes her audience laugh. And the judge lets her off.

Boccaccio's stories celebrate *ingegno*, meaning thinking on your feet with cleverness and grace. Translator Wayne A. Rebhorn notes that the tricks and wit in pursuit of sex are why *boccaccesco* in Italian is synonymous with "licentious."[15]

---

12. Boccaccio, *Decameron*, 156.

13. Boccaccio, *Decameron*, 157.

14. Boccaccio, *Decameron*, 496.

15. Rebhorn, "Introduction," xxv.

FALLING IN LOVE

The naughty stories attract us, and so does the prospect of true love. Iris Murdoch observed, "Falling in love is for many people their most intense experience, bringing with it a quasi-religious certainty, and most disturbing because it shifts the center of the world from ourself [*sic*] to another place."[16]

Consider Zoë Folbigg's personal account of love at first sight.[17]

"I can't explain it. Something about him looked like he was a good soul," she said of a fellow passenger she saw one morning on her commuter train to London. "Just something about him felt comforting and that everything was right with the world."

And he was reading García Márquez's *One Hundred Years of Solitude*, a book Zoë adored. It was a sign of connection. This too was romantic.

She told her coworkers, fellow twenty-somethings, about her crush. They nicknamed him Train Man. They urged her daily to do something, say something. She couldn't. For weeks she was on the train with him; the two never even locked eyes. After eight months, she schemed to drop a ticket on the floor near him. This would start a conversation. Heart racing, she did it. He said, "Excuse me, you dropped this"; and all she could do was squeak and move away.

Finally, two months later, she emboldened herself to write him a note. "It's my birthday," it said, "and I think everyone should do one crazy thing on their birthday and here's my thing." The note went on: She thought he looked lovely, and if he would like to have a drink with her tonight, here was her email address. If not, she wished him well and good travels.

But she just couldn't bring herself to give him the note.

This went on for over a week. Her colleagues hounded her. Finally, eleven days later, Zoë handed him the note, smiled, and walked away "as fast as my legs could take me" to the next carriage, where she slumped into a seat, feeling drained.

All that day, Zoë and her coworkers excitedly awaited a message. Nothing. Finally, at five o'clock came an email entitled "the guy on the train."

"Thank you, that was a lovely thing to do, but unfortunately I have a girlfriend." He went on to wish her well.

"It was a nice rejection," she recalled.

Zoë wondered if she should henceforth take a different train. She didn't. The next day, he and she happened to board at the same time and said hello. Both smiled, both blushed.

---

16. Murdoch, *Metaphysics as a Guide*, 16–17.
17. Folbigg, "Commuter Romance."

Life for her went on. But she was still smitten with Train Man. She went out with other people but kept asking herself why. She just wasn't interested.

Another eight months later, on a Friday she received an email from him. "If you still fancy that drink, I'd love to go out."

Zoë was delighted but mortified. She said to herself, I know I've built him up to an impossible height. This can go badly.

They met for the drink. "He really was that lovely!" She found they had humor in common, interests in common, "the same hopes and dreams."

Fast-forward: Zoë and Mark—he now had a name—went traveling together for a year. After six months, at sunset on a railway trip in rural Australia, Mark proposed. Train Man!

And, fast-forward again, twelve years later: two sons, together in love, and Zoë Folbigg published an autobiographical novel about their romance, which became a number-one bestseller in Britain.[18]

"I KNOW AND AM RIGHT FOR YOU"

"Falling in love," wrote Annie Dillard in her remarkable 2007 novel *The Maytrees*,[19] "like having a baby, rubs against the current of our lives: separation, loss and death. That is the joy of them."[20] In *The Maytrees*, true love is entwined with true sexual passion.

> It began when Lou Bigelow and Toby Maytree first met. He was back home in Provincetown after the war. Maytree first saw her on a bicycle. A red scarf, white shirt, skin clean as an eggshell, wide eyes and mouth. She stopped and leaned on a leg to talk to someone on the street. She laughed, and her loveliness caught his breath . . .
>
> He introduced himself. —You're Lou Bigelow, aren't you? She nodded. They shook hands and hers felt hot under sand like a sugar doughnut. Under her high brows she eyed him straight on and straight across. She had gone to girls' schools, he recalled later. Those girls looked straight at you. Her wide eyes, apertures opening, seem preposterously to tell him, I and these my arms are for you. I know, he thought back at the stranger, this long-limbed girl. I know and am right for you.[21]

And so Toby courted Lou, and she was quickly enthralled.

18. Folbigg, *Note*.
19. Dillard, *Maytrees*.
20. Dillard, *Maytrees*, 2.
21. Dillard, *Maytrees*, 7.

Their love soon prospered in passion. For lovemaking nearly killed Lou. Was she alright? Abashed, he held her steady until she opened her eyes. Was he a brute? What ailed her?—Whoo, she answered once, and another time, Yike. He stopped worrying. Hours afterward he used to see her, firm and young as she was, gripping the rail to check her descent downstairs.[22]

Intimacy could not be unique to her and Maytree, this brief blending, this blind sea they entered together diving. His neck smelled as suntan does, his own oil heated, and his hair smelled the same but darker. He was still fresh from an outdoor shower. Awareness was a braided river. It slid down time in drops or torrents. Now she knew he woke. The room seemed to get smarter. His legs moved and their tonus was tight. Her legs were sawdust; they were a line of old rope shreds on sand. All her life the thought of his body made her blush.[23]

Maytree, a poet, was also amazed. "Their intimacy flooded . . . their awareness rode waves paired like outriggers." He concluded Plato was misguided: "physical senses and wordless realms neither diverge nor oppose: they meet as nearest neighbors in the darkness of personality and embrace."[24]

FULFILLMENT

Beyond the intoxication of union, there can be deep meaning in finding that special, unique someone. A shared calling. The same big insight. Ways to help others, together.

Take the oh-so-bookish John Stuart Mill meeting Harriet Taylor at a dinner in 1831. He was twenty-four, she twenty-two.

Harriet was beautiful, big-eyed, with "a swan-like throat"—and oh yes, very intelligent. But married to another man since she was eighteen.

Before long, Harriet and John became inseparable—long talks, carriage rides, and, despite the disdain of scandal-sensitive friends, perhaps sexual intimacy. There is little direct evidence of the last; many of the couple's letters were later destroyed; but clearly they fell in love. Two years later, Harriet wrote John, "Far from being unhappy or even *low* this morning, I feel as tho' you had never loved me half so well as last night."[25] In 1834, Thomas Carlyle relayed the rumor that Mill had "fallen *desperately in love* with some young

22. Dillard, *Maytrees*, 38.
23. Dillard, *Maytrees*, 32.
24. Dillard, *Maytrees*, 46.
25. Robson and Stillinger, "Introduction," xvii.

philosophic beauty" and been "lost to all his friends and to himself."[26] Perhaps true of her too, as captured in this note from Harriet to John: "When I think that I shall not hold your hand until Tuesday the time is so long & my hand so useless. Adieu my delight."[27]

For Mill, being in love with that special, superior someone catalyzed his thinking and writing. In his *Autobiography*, John acknowledged how Harriet inspired his own desire to share and serve:

> Her intellectual gifts did but minister to a moral character at once the noblest and the best balanced which I have ever met with in life. Her unselfishness was not that of a taught system of duties, but of a heart which thoroughly identified itself with the feelings of others, and often went to excess in consideration for them by imaginatively investing their feelings with the intensity of its own. The passion of justice might have been thought to be her strongest feeling, but for her boundless generosity, and a lovingness ever ready to pour itself forth upon any or all human beings who were capable of giving the smallest feeling in return.[28]

BEING UNDERSTOOD

Vladimir Nabokov wrote unforgettably about *eros* and romance. In real life, too, Nabokov memorably fell in love. In May of 1923, he met Véra Slonim at a ball for the Russian émigré community of Berlin. She was twenty-one, he twenty-four.

Over the previous two years, Véra had been admiring Vladimir's work in local publications, clipping and saving his poems. That night she approached him wearing a harlequin mask of black silk. She told him she loved his writing. She explained why; he could scarcely believe it. She recited some of his poems from memory. Véra and Vladimir wandered the streets long into the night, mutually entranced.

She daringly followed up with several letters. He was overwhelmed by the audacity of sudden love and understanding. Genius captured, prodding him to do even more. He did not answer her directly, but while he was away on a trip, he published in Berlin a poem alluding to their first meeting in a way he knew that only she would capture.

26. Quoted in Sunstein, "John and Harriet."
27. Quoted in Sunstein, "John and Harriet."
28. Mill, *Autobiography and Literary Essays*, 195.

Romance and intimacy.

And then he wrote his first letter to her. It began without salutation (the ellipses are in the original):

> I won't hide it: I'm so unused to being—well, understood, per-
> haps—so unused to it, that in the very first minutes of our meet-
> ing I thought: this is a joke, a masquerade trick . . . But then . . .
> And there are things that are hard to talk about—you'll rub off
> their marvelous pollen at the touch of a word . . . They write me
> from home about mysterious flowers. You are lovely . . . And all
> your letters, too, are lovely, like the white nights.

It continued boldly: "Yes, I need you, my fairy-tale. Because you are the only person I can talk with about the shade of a cloud, about the song of a thought."[29]

Their love flourished. The next year, he wrote her: "How strange that although my life's work is moving a pen over paper, I don't know how to tell you how I love, how I desire you. Such agitation—and such divine peace: melting clouds immersed in sunshine—mounds of happiness. And I am floating with you, in you, aflame and melting . . ."[30]

From the first moments, Vladimir felt that Véra was destined to share his life. He wrote her, "It's as if in your soul there is a preprepared spot for every one of my thoughts."[31] For the next fifty-four years, he was inseparable from the brilliant, elegant woman who became Mrs. Nabokov. Among her many roles, Véra was amanuensis, translator, chief correspondent, teaching assistant, literary agent, chauffeur, Scrabble partner, and butterfly-catching companion. She was the first reader of all her husband's works, as well as critic, editor, and inspiration.[32] The dedication page of every Nabokov novel reads, "To Véra."

SEEING AND BEING SEEN

In *The Maytrees*, a "wider life" breathes in Toby: "Only the lover sees what is real, he thought . . . Far from being blind, love alone can see."[33] This point is taken up by Iris Murdoch and later, in a paper about her, by Martha Nussbaum. "One of Murdoch's major philosophical themes,"

---

29. Boyd, "Envelopes," xxvi.

30. Nabokov, *Letters to Véra*, 31–32.

31. Schiff, *Véra*, 11.

32. Acampora, "Véra Nabokov," 16.

33. Dillard, *Maytrees*, 34–5.

Nussbaum notes, was "the relationship between erotic love and the true vision of other people."[34]

When Iris Murdoch was twenty-four, she wrote to a male school friend, "Oh so much in need of intellectual intimacy. The patient mind which is prepared to comprehend my own and toss me back the ball of my thought."[35] She found some of that a few years later in Europe. She adored Parisian café life, met Sartre and Derrida, and in 1946 encountered the avant-garde French writer Raymond Queneau. Murdoch regarded Queneau as her intellectual soulmate, and her letters tell of her unrequited longing and "her final dignified settling for his friendship."[36]

But Murdoch wanted more. For her, sexual union and falling in love were personally and philosophically central. She described herself as having "an endless capacity for new loves"—including what her editors call "complex and unwise emotional imbroglios" with two of her students. An emeritus professor ended his book review of her letters this way: "One closes this astonishing volume with the thought that in her creative years the sexual act was anything but ridiculous for Iris Murdoch. Indeed, it may have been as important as writing itself."[37] Like the "amiable ladies" who heard Boccaccio's story of Alatiel, we don't quite know if the good professor suffered through Murdoch's romantic travails or sighed over them.

Murdoch certainly got the sighing part:

> Intense mutual erotic love, love which involves with the flesh all the most refined sexual being of the spirit, which reveals and perhaps even *ex nihilo* creates spirit as sex, is comparatively rare in this inconvenient world. This love presents itself as such a dizzily lofty value that even to speak of "enjoying" it seems a sacrilege. It is something to be undergone upon one's knees. And where it exists it cannot but shed a blazing light of justification upon its own scene, a light which can leave the rest of the world dark indeed.[38]

And this magic also has a philosophical valence. Murdoch speculated that romantic passion and intimacy enable a deep seeing of the other and, through love, of real presences beyond. Toward the end of her life, she returned to philosophy with a tome with the imposing title *Metaphysics as a Guide to Morals*. "We may also see how sex can be the image of spirituality as

34. Nussbaum, "Faint with Secret Knowledge," 145.

35. Murdoch, *Letters*, 126.

36. Horner and Rowe, "Introduction," xii.

37. Sutherland, "Living on Paper."

38. Murdoch, *Sacred and Profane Love Machine*, 261

well as its substance . . . A love relationship can occasion extreme selfishness and possessive violence, the attempt to dominate that other place so that it can be no longer separate; or it can prompt a process of unselfing wherein the lover learns to see, and cherish and respect, what is not himself."[39]

This "unselfing" is not the meek dimming and withdrawal of one's own desires and needs. Rather, it refers a deep sense that Another is primal. With mystics, it is God and creation. In romantic intimacy, Murdoch says, it is the person loved.

THE GLORIES AND DESECRATIONS OF LOVE

One more time: "wherein the lover learns to see, and cherish and respect, what is not himself." What a wonderful dimension of romantic love. And as we have seen, there is more:

- mutual love with a person who "just makes the world seem right";

- sexual union that turns your legs into "sawdust, a line of old rope shreds on sand";

- being seen and understood, "as if in your soul there is a preprepared spot for every one of my thoughts";

- encountering the beloved so deeply that you are "unselfed";

- forging an intimate partnership to pursue a calling, together.

Chorus: "You are lovely; you are admirable! I am awed! And you see me; you understand! I see you, and through you, so much more! All of this, all of you, inspires me to create a fuller human life!"

Bravo!

But one more time, too, from Murdoch: "A love relationship can occasion extreme selfishness and possessive violence, the attempt to dominate." Even in Murdoch's own novels. "Above all, she was superb at portraying the madness of love and the way it can transform ordinary people into crazed and possessive beings."[40] Many of Murdoch's real-life sexual forays sound anything but heroic. Many of *The Decameron*'s stories end like sexy fairy tales, but translator Wayne A. Rebhorn notes that sadism may lie in wait: romantic passion sometimes contains, or becomes, the urge to harm and humiliate.[41]

---

39. Murdoch, *Metaphysics*, 16–7.

40. Horner and Rowe, "Introduction," xiii.

41. Rebhorn, "Introduction," xliv.

These days, sexual predators fill the news and social media. Their victims, in the beginning perhaps flattered by attention from a powerful man, end up spiritually and sometimes physically injured. Not loved, but exploited; not enthralled, but disgusted; not uplifted, but degraded. And some of the "patterns of predation, especially in the cases of Weinstein and C. K., have a grotesqueness that discourages fantasy." "These men exposed and pleasured themselves in front of horrified women. Restate what they did, and it sounds like the worst sex life you could aspire to: frantically trapping people in a room, people who are disgusted to be there, while you engage in the most arid form of sexual pleasure possible."[42]

No wonder Thomas à Kempis was worried.

Thomas probably didn't ask the monks to focus their Bible studies on Solomon's Song of Songs. In fact, if Audible did the Bible, that new "Take Me to the Good Part" feature might jump, with a breathy female narrator, to Song of Songs 7:11–13:

> [11] Come, my love, let's go to the field; let's spend the night among the henna blossoms.
> [12] Let's go early to the vineyards; let's see if the vine has budded, if the blossom has opened, if the pomegranates are in bloom. There I will give you my love.
> [13] The mandrakes give off a fragrance, and at our doors is every delicacy—new as well as old. I have treasured them up for you, my love.

Thomas commanded his charges to spurn the vineyards and mandrakes. For him and his monks, chastity was the solution to the desecrations of romantic love. The apostle Paul was asked if people should abstain from sex. Best, he replied, to be chaste like me—unless you can't control yourself, in which case get married so that you don't just "burn with passion."[43]

That's the ascetic line. Our stylized addict responds: Nonsense, get as much as you can. Demystify romantic love, enjoy "zipless sex."[44] The male addict may dream of the avatar in the 2017 film *Blade Runner 2049*: an Ana de Armas who reads you and then morphs to exactly the person you need right now, and even grows to love you. The avatar who is your "Cool Girl":

42. Sargeant, "Consent."

43. 1 Corinthians 7:1–9.

44. Apologies to Erica Jong for toning down her epic phrase, which urbandictionary.com defines as "a sexual encounter between strangers that has the swift compression of a dream and is seemingly free of all remorse and guilt. It is absolutely pure, there is no power game and it is free of ulterior motives." Erica Jong's character liked the idea, but "it is rarer than the unicorn. And I have never had one." Jong, *Fear of Flying*, 21–22.

Hot and understanding. Cool Girls never get angry; they only smile in a chagrined, loving manner and let their men do whatever they want . . . It may be a slightly different version—maybe he's a vegetarian, so Cool Girl loves seitan and is great with dogs; or maybe he's a hipster artist, so Cool Girl is a tattooed, bespectacled nerd who loves comics. There are variations to the window dressing, but believe me, he wants Cool Girl, who is basically the girl who likes everything he likes and doesn't ever complain.[45]

Or Cool Guy.

But the hero's flourishing life avoids these extremes. It neither spurns the world nor voraciously elevates worldly experiences to ultimate goals. In the world yet outside himself (or herself), the stylized hero is magnified by his calling, defined by his insight, and fully engaged with us in sharing and service. Just so for romantic love as well. Murdoch's philosophical treatise *The Sovereignty of Good* argues that "We need a moral philosophy in which the concept of love, so rarely mentioned now by philosophers, can once again be made central."[46] The narrator of Murdoch's novel *The Black Prince* says, "Love sees truly, in part, because it *does* see divinity rather than the muddled everyday."[47] In Platonic terms that Thomas à Kempis might appreciate, *The Sovereignty of Good* talks about the flourishing life as one that sees the Good. The Good is metaphorically like the sun, metaphorically a magnetic center. We can discern light coming from the sun, and through iron shavings the forces of a magnetic field, but we "do not and probably cannot know, conceptualize, what it is like in the center."[48]

There is a way to get there, "though one rarely mentioned by our contemporary philosophers, and that is Love."[49] Including, as always for Iris Murdoch, romantic love and intimacy.

She sees the risks of romantic love and intimacy but warrants its glories: "[Love] is capable of infinite degradation and is the source of our greatest errors; but when it is even partially refined it is the energy and passion of the soul in its search for Good, the force that joins us to Good and joins

---

45. Lightly edited quotation from the film *Gone Girl* (2014), cited in Rothfeld, "Gone Girl."

46. Murdoch, *Sovereignty*, 45.

47. Nussbaum, "'Faint with Secret Knowledge,'" 148.

48. Murdoch, *Sovereignty*, 32–33.

49. Murdoch, *Sovereignty*, 99.

us to the world through Good. Its existence is the unmistakable sign that
we are spiritual creatures, attracted by excellence and made for the Good."[50]

A GIFT

It is the purity of our effort in love that matters, not our prowess or the
radius of our talents and influence. When we receive the gift of love, we feel
deep down that it is all right for us to be imperfect, all right to be human
beings, all right to be confused about what to do and how.

In Lewis Hyde's remarkable book *The Gift*, true artists welcome their
creative gifts—both talent and "a specific intuition or inspiration"—and in
turn impart gifts of art. To Hyde, the trajectory of art is receiving and giving,
receiving again and giving again. Although there exist objects of art that are
bought and sold, just as there exist sex objects, their commodification does
violence to the artistic spirit, just as it does to romantic love and intimacy.
Recall the "lofty" married lady in *The Decameron* who gave away in love her
extra helpings of passion. After her acquittal, the story concludes, the town's
law on adultery was changed to forbid only the sale of sex, not receiving it
or giving it away.

"A gift is a thing we do not get by our own efforts," Hyde insisted. "We
cannot acquire it through an act of will. It is bestowed upon us . . . Although
a talent can be perfected through an effort of the will, no effort in the world
can cause its initial appearance."[51] The same goes for the gift of romance and
intimacy.[52] The jolt and surprise of romantic love, its physicality and yet its
transporting otherworldliness, its radical *unselfing*, are signs and metaphors
for meaning in life. In *The Maytrees*, the transcendence of sexual intimacy
is so wondrous as to confound. "Love so sprang at her, she honestly thought
no one had ever looked into it. Where was it in literature? Someone would

50. Murdoch, *Sovereignty*, 100.

51. Hyde, *Gift*, xiv.

52. Recall how Abraham Maslow described "self-actualized lives": "One can fairly
use the old words vocation, or calling, or mission to describe their passionate, selfless,
and profound feeling for their 'work' . . . I hesitate to call this simply 'purposefulness'
because that may imply that it happens only out of will, purpose, decision, or calculation,
and doesn't give enough weight to the subjective feeling of being swept along, of willing
and eager surrender, or yielding to fate and happily embracing it at the same time . . .
The best way to communicate these feelings to someone who doesn't intuitively, directly
understand them is to use as a model 'falling in love.' This is clearly different from doing
one's duty, or doing what is sensible and logical. And clearly also 'will,' if mentioned at all,
is used in a very special sense. And when two people love each other fully, then each one
knows what it feels like to be a magnet and what it feels like to be iron filings, and what it
feels like to be both simultaneously." Maslow, *Farther Reaches*, 301, 303.

have written something. She must not have recognized it. Time to read everything again."[53]

Time to read everything again, together; and to create something new, together. The lover, like the artist, takes risks, embraces life's transience and the real presences beyond, and creates something unique and beautiful.

And we don't have to be Vladimir Nabokov or Harriet Taylor, nor the lofty lady or Zoë Folbigg. Romantic love goes right when we gratefully allow it to manifest itself in our calling, our insight, and our sharing and service. Whoever we are.

53. Dillard, *Maytrees*, 31.

PART IV

Recurrence

10

Backsliding

Suppose you have stood up to upheaval and are ready to make life-defining decisions. You have reconsidered your calling, sought big insights, and embraced the goals of sharing and serving. You have rethought romance and intimacy in your life, including the possibility that you and your beloved can share a calling, be inspired by the same big ahas, and go forth in the world to impart your gifts with others.

Now we consider the possibility that all these good things go sour.

For one thing, new external shocks can create new upheavals. These, in turn, can shake your calling, crack your big insight, and make your methods of sharing and serving seem inane. But in this chapter we'll consider a more common, more gradual way that your purpose, meaning, and action channels can be undermined: backsliding.

Let's begin with some examples from politics and policy, and then we'll turn to everyday challenges.

WHAT IS BACKSLIDING?

Around the world, we hear that democracy is in danger. One phenomenon is the violent overthrow of at least nominally democratic regimes, such as Afghanistan. That's not backsliding, though—that's cataclysm.

More common, in the opinion of many political scientists, is the gradual erosion of democratic norms and institutions. "Backsliding," write David Waldner and Eleanor Lust, "makes elections less competitive without entirely undermining the electoral mechanism; it restricts participation without explicitly abolishing norms of universal franchise seen as constitutive of contemporary democracy; and it loosens constraints of accountability by eroding norms of answerability and punishment."[1]

In their book *How Democracies Die*, Steven Levitsky and Daniel Ziblatt describe an incremental demise. "Because there is no single moment—no coup, declaration of martial law, or suspension of the constitution—in which the regime obviously 'crosses the line' into dictatorship, nothing may set off society's alarm bells. Those who denounce government abuse may be dismissed as exaggerating or crying wolf. Democracy's erosion is, for many, almost imperceptible."[2]

What to do? You have to be strong, and you have to take sustained steps to keep strong. David G. Timberman notes that democratic backsliding is more likely in "low-quality democracies like the Philippines, where concerted and sustained efforts are required to improve the quality of democracy. Absent that, backsliding is inevitable."[3]

Note this: when democratic backsliding occurs, it's not because the people or the leaders have disavowed what we might call the democratic calling of "government by, for, and of the people." Few are rejecting the big insight of giving "two cheers for democracy" because it is the imperfect but salutary antidote to tyranny and corruption. And yet, the calling and the insight can slide away.

Speaking of corruption, we often see backsliding here as well. Recently my graduate class considered the case of Colombia. In 1998, a new president arrived in the midst of economic recession, civil unrest, cocaine trafficking galore, and widespread corruption. He tackled the corruption in remarkable ways. In 1998, Colombia was ranked at the 6th percentile in the Corruption Perceptions Index. By 2005, it was at the 65th percentile. Our class studied how Colombia did it.

But then we looked at backsliding. By 2018, Colombia had retrogressed to the 45th percentile on the Corruption Perceptions Index. According to the World Economic Forum's Global Competitiveness Index, in 2019 Colombia ranked 80th of 141 countries in "incidence of corruption," tied with Brazil and Indonesia, worse than Albania, Ghana, and India. Dramatic incidents showed that the battle against corruption had waned. In June 2017, the head of the anti-corruption unit within the office of the attorney general was arrested for accepting bribes and laundering money. His cooperation

1. Waldner and Lust, "Unwelcome Change," 95.
2. Levitsky and Ziblatt, *How Democracies Die*, 5–6.
3. Timberman, *Philippine Politics under Duterte*.

subsequently led to investigations or indictments of three supreme court justices as well as multiple legislators and officials.

Colombia had declared itself against corruption, enacted new policies, and succeeded in reducing corruption. There was popular support. And yet, a new government in the same country slid backwards. No one declared, "Okay, let's get back to corruption." In fact, the rhetoric of honest governance still blared out at every political meeting and in every presidential speech. But backsliding happened.

It also happens in other areas of public policy. Consider hyperinflation, when rates of inflation get into the hundreds of percent per year.[4] Hyperinflation is a disaster for medium-term investment of all kinds, leading to economic collapse. One of the few things economists know is how to address serious inflation. Stop printing money, slow down the emission of credit. And yet, some countries that have successfully halted hyperinflation have reverted to it.

Why? Debts denominated in the local currency are cheaper to repay. Social security payments and other programs to help those in need are more easily funded, at least in nominal terms. Short-run political benefits may ensue. But taken too far, inflationary policies can hypertrophy. A drug may make our cares today go away but lead to a harmful addiction. So too with inflation.

For another example of backsliding, consider Ecuador and malaria. This South American country has eradicated malaria three times. Wait, how can something be eradicated more than once? If it's gone, it's gone. If the conditions for mosquito breeding are not watched with care, those hateful insects will migrate back in and reestablish themselves. Governments, like people, find it easier to pronounce reforms and to initiate them with fanfare than to maintain reforms through the undramatic daily disciplines of upkeep and renewal.

BACKSLIDING IN EVERYDAY LIFE

These examples have analogies in our personal lives. We loudly announce our new fitness program and pay to join that gym. We make progress. But within a year, or sadly a couple of months, our ardor flags, our old habits resume. We backslide.

So it goes with dieting, watching television, surfing the web, avoiding that second drink—and, in more concerning behaviors, fighting addictions. "The relapse of problem behavior after apparently successful treatment,"

4. Marcet and Nicolini, "Recurrent Hyperinflations and Learning."

write Duncan Pritchard, Marguerite Hoerger, and F. Charles Mace, "is an enduring problem for the field of applied behavior analysis."[5]

Aristotle called it *akrasia*, defined as uncompelled intentional behavior that is contrary to the agent's better judgment.[6] The phenomenon is captured in the apostle Paul's lament, "I do not understand what I do. For what I want to do I do not do, but what I hate I do."[7]

The Nobel laureate economist Thomas C. Schelling studied how to prevent and overcome backsliding. It is, he said, as though each of us contains different selves—one wanting to exercise, the other not—locked in "an intimate battle of self-command."[8] In a moment, we'll consider some of his tips. For now, let's note that backsliding does not happen because we change our goals or our minds. Democracy erodes, corruption reemerges, and hyperinflation recurs even though people say they value democracy, abhor corruption, and understand that hyperinflation is bad. So too with efforts to quit smoking, lose weight, and halt procrastination. Lapses and relapses. Backsliding.

BACKSLIDING IN OUR CALLINGS AND INSIGHTS

Backsliding can happen with what really matters. Even if you don't necessarily renounce your calling, you may in some sense forget it. You don't disown your big insight; you allow it to slip your mind.

A few years ago, the satirical magazine *The Onion* had a story about an "area man" who, while driving home, suddenly had an epiphany that made sense of his whole life. But before he arrived home, he'd forgotten what it was (see Box 6.)

You may recall from college days learning something, mastering it to the point of getting that A, and a month after the final exam finding your "learning" was, shall we say, *hard to access.*

In other words, we forget. Even what our transcript says we've learned.

Friedrich Nietzsche once remarked that forgetfulness has its upside. "The advantage of a bad memory is that one can enjoy the same good things for the first time *several* times."[9]

---

5. Pritchard et al., "Treatment Relapse," 814.

6. Meanwhile, *enkrateia* is the opposite, namely, self-control, continence, strength of will. See Mele, *Backsliding.*

7. Romans 7:15.

8. Schelling, "Intimate Contest."

9. Nietzsche, *Human, All Too Human*, §580.

BOX 6. LIFE-CHANGING EPIPHANY
WEARS OFF ON RIDE HOME

ALBUQUERQUE, NM—Despite being overcome by a profound realization just minutes earlier that challenged his long-held beliefs and promised to forever alter his daily existence, sources confirmed that 42-year-old Thomas Wilson's epiphany had fully worn off during his drive home Wednesday. The deeply affecting and eye-opening revelation, which in an instant had caused him to completely reassess his priorities, was reportedly pushed to the back of Wilson's mind as he stopped to fill up his car with gas, fading to just a fraction of its initial impact moments later as he began listening to a podcast on his vehicle's stereo system. According to reports, as Wilson shifted his focus to navigating road construction and merging onto a particularly busy stretch of highway, the last shred of his momentous eureka moment had nearly dissolved away. At press time, the life-changing insight was fully extinguished as Wilson walked in through his front door and discovered the latest Hammacher Schlemmer catalogue waiting in his mail.[10]

But for learning, maybe not such an advantage.

What about for callings? What about big insights? What about sharing and serving?

How can erosion attack a peak experience that leads to a revaluation of life? Is there something in our nature that reaches heights of insight and knowledge, revelation and hope, love and rapture—only to slide down from those heights, sometimes ignominiously as in the crash of tulip mania, sometimes as with democratic backsliding "so slowly and incrementally that at any moment people hardly notice"?

A few years ago, I read a touching account by a middle-aged Christian woman of attending a convention of college-age evangelicals. She was caught up in their fervor and joy, and then melancholy set in. "I used to be that convicted and committed," she thought. "What happened?"

You see similar things with physicians wondering what happened to their passion for medicine and for helping others. With teachers and social workers. Alas, with lovers and with family members. "What happened?"

---

10. "Life-Changing Epiphany."

"Age happened," I suppose is one answer. As with the bodies of athletes or appetites for adventure, some say that passions predictably dim with age. "Enthusiasm belongs to the outgoing cycle of life" that is youth, Eckhart Tolle declares. And as you age, "It is only through surrender that you can align yourself with the return movement—the journey home."[11] One's calling or big insight, be it secular or spiritual, may come to seem an obsolete product of the past.

What can be done? One idea is to fight back. Insight, passion, awe—they are still available to us. And so human beings everywhere have invented disciplines, techniques, reminders to prevent or overcome backsliding.

ANTI-BACKSLIDING

Back to Thomas Schelling and "self-command." To prevent backsliding, we must keep ourselves from taking a course that is convenient but not what we really want. The paradox is apparent: "we don't want to do what we do" is nonsense to some hard-core economists. But take smoking behavior: the majority of smokers say they would like to quit but don't. Schelling analyzed this apparent contradiction as if each of us were two separate persons, bargaining against one another.

Self 1 wants to quit smoking. But Self 2 readily and predictably succumbs to temptation. Knowing that, Self 1 takes preventive measures. Don't have any cigarettes in the house. Don't go places where others are smoking. Make big bets enforceable by others that you won't smoke for a month. Take antagonists to nicotine, reducing the pleasure of smoking. Join forces with others trying to quit to reinforce the commitment, enhance accountability, and create rewards for succeeding.

One can reinforce the desire to quit by providing information about smoking's health risks or its unattractiveness to romantic partners. (One ad said, "Kissing a smoker is like licking an ashtray.") Role models and success stories also can help, including firsthand accounts of how they quit and how happy they are that they did.

Disciplines and habits are other devices to ward off backsliding. It's easier to exercise if we create routines and have workout partners. Some students may ask for regular homework assignments even though they don't like homework, because they recognize how temptations can crowd out studying. One of the most successful teachers of the case method used "cold calls," meaning the professor would suddenly asked a random student

---

11. Tolle, *New Earth*, 304.

for an analysis. Both he and his initially uncomfortable students attested to better preparation, enhanced learning, and higher course ratings.

Consider the roles of rules and disciplines in religion. Apostasy happens, but backsliding is the more common threat to people's spiritual callings. Some of the same countermeasures Schelling studied emerge here. Small groups and regular meetings or services create something like deadlines, with external as well as internal accountability. Rituals and rites evoke the feelings and convey the insights. Spiritual disciplines represent in their austerity and visibility a commitment that others can observe and potentially enforce. Rules and regulations can guide large and small actions and activities, at first enhancing and undergirding behavior that faith says we should perform out of love, and then, alas, crowding out the love.

In religious contexts, prayer and scripture can bolster resilience against backsliding. As a senior in high school, I attended a Jesuit school in Spain. Mass every morning, Rosary every afternoon. As the only Protestant in the school—the only American to boot—I was not expected to participate fully. Many of the boys would blast through those Hail Marys. The priest would sometimes admonish them: "Slow down, boys; think about the words you're saying." To many of them it was an empty practice, I'm sure. But I remember it affectionately. I liked and still like the spirit of it—devoting time every morning and afternoon as part of the routine. And I found, myself, time to reflect and maybe even be restored.

I love a line from Marilynne Robinson: "First reverence, then belief."[12] Prayer gives us a chance to revere God. So does reverence for nature itself—if we can be still and reflective in its beauty and complexity. Our very busyness can lead to backsliding and despair[13]; meditation can be an antidote.

The regular reading of scripture is a practice in most world religions. Individuals have *their* scriptures, the ones that helped convict and convert them. But, as with the eight reasons or the fundamental theorems we have forgotten, we may no longer have this passage, that argument, this concordance fresh in our minds. Reading them again, we may even have that Nietzschean surprise of encountering familiar texts as if for the first time. In a different way than the first time, and in some sense as different people, we may reexperience conversion.

12. Robinson, "Credo," 22.

13. "By seeing the multitude of men about it, by getting engaged in all sorts of worldly affairs, by becoming wise about how things go in this world, such a man forgets himself, forgets what his name is (in the divine understanding of it), does not dare to believe in himself, finds it too venturesome a thing to be himself, far easier and safer to be like the others, to become an imitation, a number, a cipher in the crowd. This form of despair is hardly ever noticed in the world." Kierkegaard, *Sickness unto Death*, 166–67.

Now let's take these points beyond a religious context. Through practices of self-command, through something akin to meditation and the re-reading of our formative texts, our callings and insights can be renewed. But we may not do these things even though we say we wish to. We may backslide. Enter here the roles of disciplines and habits, of fellow pilgrims and practitioners who can hold us to account.

WHEN PREVENTING BACKSLIDING
BECOMES PART OF THE PROBLEM

But here let us note a deep irony, if not a contradiction. A component of that big aha! of conversion—in religion and also, I believe, regarding many secular conversion experiences à la Kuhn and the big insights we considered earlier—is a sudden recognition that our disciplines and habits have become the problem. Religious rules and practices, alas, can *get in the way* of salvation. Can *substitute* for grace and compassion. Can *stand between* us and God.

A theme in many faith traditions is the adept hero who denounces practices that have become ossified and sages who have become Pharisees. One revered figure in Mahayana Buddhism is the twelve-year-old princess who derided hypocritical monks as "jackals" (and more). In Bhutan, there is a beloved character from centuries ago called the "Divine Madman." He mastered Buddhist scriptures and practices as a young man, then went off on remarkable adventures and romantic exploits—only to end up in the most sacred of monasteries teasing and debating the most learned of savants, and defeating them.[14]

Jesus's remarkable outbursts in Matthew 23 epitomize this theme. He condemns the teachers of the law and the Pharisees, who meticulously enforce all the rules and regulations but neglect "the more important matters of the law—justice, mercy, and faithfulness." His vilifications are vivid. The Pharisees are hypocrites; they are "whitewashed tombs, which look beautiful on the outside but on the inside are full of the bones of the dead and everything unclean." They are snakes, a brood of vipers. They are killers of the prophets and sages and teachers.

Even devout practices and the most thorough mastery of the canon, then, can have the paradoxical quality of defeating the original calling and undermining the original insight. People like the Divine Madman then show up—masters, not outside critics—and their example and outside-the-canon behavior upset but invigorate the status quo. In many cultures and

14. Monson and Tshering, *More Than a Madman*.

traditions, there are in-between figures who go from the chaotic world to the heavenly realms and back again, leaving the world wiser, the heavens looser, and both ready to create anew. Following others, Lewis Hyde calls them "tricksters," but he admits that a more accurate though unwieldy name might be "Trickster-Transformer-Culture Hero."[15]

Can we be tricksters and transformers when our callings and insights start to constrain what they were designed to enable? Intellectually, can we transit back and forth, as did the mature Thomas Kuhn, between two seemingly incompatible views: (1) scientific theories are socially embedded and therefore relativistic and (2) science nonetheless progresses because new, objective facts prove some theories to be better predictors than others?

Can we recognize with Marilynne Robinson that both (1) the laws of physics and astronomy explain the patterns of light and dark we observe and (2) God's presence may in those same phenomena be apprehended? When she was in college, Robinson received a big aha! that lasted the rest of her life.

> I went to the library and read an assigned text, Jonathan Edwards's *Doctrine of Original Sin Defended*. There is a long footnote in this daunting treatise that discusses the light of the moon, and how the apparent continuing of the moon's light is a consequence of its reflecting light that is in fact continuously renewed. This was Edwards's analogy for the continuous renewal of the world by the will of God, which creates, to our eyes, seeming lawfulness and identity, but which is in fact a continuous free act of God . . . Edwards's footnote was . . . my escape, and what an escape it was, from the contending, tedious determinisms that seemed to be all that was on offer to me then . . . By grace of that footnote, I realized that I could think of God as present and intentional, and of reality as essentially addressed to human perception—perception being then as now my greatest interest and pleasure in life.[16]

Can we say *both* that all callings are socially embedded and psychologically conditioned *and* that each of us has the agency to make better choices of callings?

Both/and can prevent the stultification of our insights and practices—or help us cope with it if it occurs. We can use meditation and revered texts to cue up the best of who we were and use them to reexamine where we have now arrived.

15. Hyde, *Trickster Makes This World*, 7n.
16. Robinson, "Credo," 27.

PRESERVING AND RENEWING

Sadly, it is all too human to forget our callings, trivialize our insights. Para-doxically, perhaps, research on addiction may shed light on how to preserve and renew them.

Many if not most addicts wish to quit. They understand the costs and have a correct perspective on the benefits. They resolve, "That's it—enough. No more drugs."

But that's in the morning. That night the addict goes to his usual club. There he is exposed to what economists B. Douglas Bernheim and Antonio Rangel call "cues."[17] The cues may be a certain setting with familiar music, smoke, and other people getting high. Suddenly, a metaphorical switch in the addict's brain flips, and he is a different person: in economic parlance, he suddenly behaves as if he is maximizing a different utility function. The addict falls off the wagon and indulges.

Later, when his high is over, the addict often laments his decision to take a hit. It is not quite that he was acting irrationally—rather, that he was acting rationally by a different utility function that he, in his normal mode, rejects. The cues then become part of the problem—and part of the solution. They are part of Schelling's "self-command": "People avoid cues and precursors, the sights and smells that subvert their abstinent intentions; people dare not eat the first peanut, start an argument, begin the novel they can't afford to take the time to read, or turn on the TV because it is harder to turn off than merely not to turn on."[18]

Let's apply this idea in a positive vein: not to cues that drive us to addiction, but to cues that rekindle our callings and insights. How might positive cues metaphorically switch our brains back to the better people that, upon reflection and commitment, we wish to try to be?

Let's cue up Reinhold Neibuhr for some inspiration—but take a deep breath first and take his remarks beyond their religious context to the broader spaces of purpose and meaning.

> The general revelation of personal human experience, the sense of being confronted with a "wholly other" at the edge of human consciousness, contains three elements, two of which are not too sharply defined, while the third is not defined at all. The first is the sense of reverence for a majesty and of dependence upon an ultimate source of being. The second is the sense of moral obligation laid upon one from beyond oneself and of moral

17. Bernheim and Rangel, "Addiction and Cues."

18. Schelling, "Ethics, Law," 65. See also Schelling, "Intimate Contest" and "Self-Command."

unworthiness before a judge. The third, most problematic of the elements in religious experience, is the longing for forgiveness.[19]

Let's play with the idea of *positive cues* using Niebuhr's framework as an example. How might we prompt ourselves to evoke reverence, moral obligation and unworthiness, and a longing for forgiveness?

Majesty

You know what they say about lived experience—each person's is different. For you, what cues that feeling of *majesty and dependence*? Can you evoke it through thirty minutes of gazing at the constellations? Or with a hike to the top of a mountain and then sitting there and staring out, with a wild surmise, at the nature you partake in? Or can you imbibe a profound and noble study in history, or archaeology, or science, and then reflect gratefully upon the fact that it exists? Can you beckon something outside yourself that enables you to perceive deeply, and be awed by, life's beauty, complexity, and mystery?

Moral Obligation

What might be a cue for you for feelings of *moral obligation and moral unworthiness*? Perhaps moral outrage is a start—outrage over cruelty, dehumanization, or the mistreatment of the environment. That's familiar, perhaps all too familiar; I think it's only a start. Outrage may often lead to blaming others and condemning the system, rather than to inspiring and changing yourself. Niebuhr's point is to focus on your own moral obligations and, what he provocatively puts in the same breath, your own moral unworthiness. How might you evoke those feelings?

Forgiveness

Finally, what do you associate with a feeling that you want or need *forgiveness*? Niebuhr calls that feeling a "longing." Can you recall having a longing for forgiveness? When? What were the accompaniments? How might you cue that feeling again?

19. Niebuhr, *Nature and Destiny*, 131.

SUSTAINABLE CONVERSIONS

The fact that democratic backsliding occurs is depressing because people everywhere say they want democracy. When corruption arises again after being condemned and at least partially thwarted, we may easily become cynical. Our old friends Bail and Flail reemerge.

So too when we see committed careers neglected, "my most important job is being a parent" let slide, and a moral identity become at best a pretense, at worst a memory. The fact that backsliding occurs among religious converts is also dispiriting (if you'll pardon the term). If through conversion people are new men and women, with new values and beliefs, then their backsliding to being old men and women makes one ask, "What does a new calling mean if it's not sustainable? What is a big and glorious aha! if it fades?"

William James had an interesting answer.

> One word, before I close this lecture, on the question of the transiency or permanence of these abrupt conversions. Some of you, I feel sure, knowing that numerous backslidings and relapses take place, make of these their apperceiving mass for interpreting the whole subject, and dismiss it with a pitying smile at so much "hysterics." Psychologically, as well as religiously, however, this is shallow. It misses the point of serious interest, which is not so much the duration as the nature and quality of these shiftings of character to higher levels. Men lapse from every level—we need no statistics to tell us that. Love is, for instance, well known not to be irrevocable, yet, constant or inconstant, it reveals new flights and reaches of ideality while it lasts. These revelations form its significance to men and women, whatever be its duration. So with the conversion experience: that it should for even a short time show a human being what the high-water mark of his spiritual capacity is, this is what constitutes its importance—an importance which backsliding cannot diminish, although persistence might increase it.[20]

These points resonate beyond religion. If you have ever felt a calling or had a big insight click but seen it lapse, go back to the key texts and experiences that got you there. Feel that flow again. Listen to those old symphonies that inspired you, revisit the rural development project where you used to

---

20. James, *Varieties of Religious Experience*, 252. James goes on to be more optimistic about even faded conversion experiences. "As a matter of fact, all the more striking instances of conversion, all those, for instance, which I have quoted, *have* been permanent . . . 'the persons who have passed through conversion, having once taken a stand for the religious life, tend to feel themselves identified with it, no matter how much their religious enthusiasm declines.'" James, *Varieties of Religious Experience*, 252, 253.

work, or spend two days in your favorite museum. Attend a weekend retreat with people who are fired up with that calling and insight. Or get off by yourself to ponder, wander, recall, and rejuvenate. And then perhaps you can, slowly but surely, get back on a schedule of doing what you used to do effortlessly, and see what happens.

11

Your Full Human Life

When our lives and our world are in upheaval, we may recoil to extremes. We may renounce the world and go into hiding. Or we may grab the world, renouncing every limit on our greed. As the poet Lisa Wells notes, "When a person has a problem with numbing or checking out, violence, drunkenness, sex, hallucination, whatever—extremes can be very seductive, as a strategy to feel and to locate a boundary."

Wells's 2021 book *Believers* is about people who avoid these extremes, "people who have suffered painful traumas and have found ways to reconcile with that history, and now devote their lives to bringing reconciliation into the world. There's no abstraction, there's nothing really—and I don't mean for this to sound anti-intellectual—but there's nothing really academic about it. It's like, 'I survived and therefore I will help others.'"[1]

Because of the world's "violence, drunkenness, hallucination, whatever," one reaction is to renounce it and flee into solitude. Thomas à Kempis advised his monks, "Learn now to die to the world, that you may begin to live with Christ. Learn now to despise all earthly things, that you may go freely to Christ."[2]

In contrast, the stylized addict renounces restrictions on his or her worldliness. Those ideals we've embraced, the ways we've been taught to

---

1. Wells, *Believers*. The quote is from Juliani, "Lisa Wells."
2. Kempis, *Imitation of Christ*, 59.

behave, are false prophets. Reinder Ganzevoort called this reaction to crisis "a negative conversion," that is, away from religion toward society.[3]

Like the solitary ascetic, the extreme addict may end up alone, away from the world, in a kind of living death. "In late stage addiction . . . the desiring self largely drops out the picture, as the addicted individual begins to mindlessly consume. This impairment is clinically significant because the machinery of motivated rationality has become corrupted."[4]

The hero engages with the world in a very different way. The hero discovers or receives a calling, finds or is given an insight, feels gratitude, and then shares and serves.

The ascetic bails. The addict flails. The hero prevails.

Apart from the heroes of myth and legend, of history and religion, we see this pattern in our midst. We find humble heroes in our companies and social movements, our fields of study and our favorite sports, and in our families and peers.[5] In surveys, most people respond that they have heroes. Some are the big heroes, with a capital H. Others are everyday heroes, people they know who exemplify "a concern for other people in need—a concern to defend a moral cause, knowing there is a personal risk, done without expectation of reward."[6] Some social critics contend that ours is an anti-heroic or post-heroic age, that "heroism has lost meaning with modernization. Against this, empirical studies point to hero-worship in today's societies, suggesting that claims of a corrosion of heroism are (at best) exaggerated."[7]

Anne Colby and William Damon tried to understand "moral exemplars," people who discovered a calling, embraced it, and then spent their lives sharing and serving. These people did not escape from the world or from themselves. "It is not so much that they overcome their fears, doubts, or resentments over the risks and hardships in their lives; it is more that they treasure the chance to take them on. The exemplars create for themselves a world of certainty rather than doubt, a perspective of faith rather than despair."[8] They felt and believed in their callings. "It is a picture of striking joy, great certainty, and unremitting faith; one that results in both high standards for the self and charity toward others."[9]

3. Ganzevoort, "Crisis Experiences," 28.

4. Matthews, "Chronic Automaticity," 199.

5. Worthington and Allison, *Heroic Humility*.

6. Zimbardo, "What Makes a Hero?"

7. Frisk, "Social Structuring of Heroism," 98.

8. Colby and Damon, *Some Do Care*, xii.

9. Colby and Damon, *Some Do Care*, 5.

David Bornstein studied activist heroes who engaged fervently with a crazy world. Each of them had a hero, someone close to them with "outstandingly strong values." And at some point a combination of an upheaval and their own preparation yielded a transformative decision away from their former lives. What fascinated Bornstein most "is the way they hold to an internal vision no matter how many disruptive forces surround them. Somehow they find ways to construct meanings for themselves and hold to those meanings. On a daily basis, they manage to align their interests, abilities and beliefs, while acting to produce changes that are deeply meaningful."[10]

Abraham Maslow was awestruck by two of his own real-life heroes.

> I could not be content simply to adore, but sought to understand why these two people were so different from the run-of-the-mill people of the world. These two people were Ruth Benedict and Max Wertheimer . . . When I tried to understand them, think about them, and write about them in my journal and my notes, I realized in one wonderful moment that their two patterns could be generalized. I was talking about a kind of person, not about two noncomparable individuals. There was remarkable excitement in that. I tried to see whether this pattern could be found elsewhere, and I did find it elsewhere, in one person after another.[11]

What is the pattern among these heroes? They have a calling: they are motivated by values and things outside themselves.[12] They have enthusiasm that ranges wide, and yet is not goofy.[13] It's part of a dialectic, a seriousness. They experience fully, without self-consciousness.[14] They are fully aware of the here and now. Yes, they do lots of hard work to be prepared for discernment,[15] and yet their big insights and peak experiences are not the result of hard work—they are like gifts. These people are creative.[16] The love they have for what they do, and for people around them, are what enables them to contribute deeply.[17]

What is the antithesis of these self-actualizing heroes? "The superficial, the moment-bound, the here-bound ones, those who are totally absorbed

---

10. Bornstein, *Change the World*, 279.

11. Maslow, *Farther Reaches*, 40–41.

12. Maslow, *Farther Reaches*, 43.

13. Maslow, *Farther Reaches*, 92.

14. Maslow, *Farther Reaches*, 45, 65–66.

15. Maslow, *Farther Reaches*, 48.

16. Maslow, *Farther Reaches*, 68, 93–94.

17. Maslow, *Farther Reaches*, 17.

with the trivial, those who are 'plated with piety, not alloyed with it,' those who are reduced to the concrete, to the momentary, and to the immediately selfish."[18]

HEROISM IN THE LARGE AND THE SMALL

We ordinary people seem to confront heroism only at a distance. We are not heroes like saints or soldiers. Nonetheless, the steps in the heroic path may serve as a kind of practical method for self-improvement. Let's play with that idea at two levels: in the large and in the small.

In the large refers to our transformative decisions about the way we're going to live our lives. When faced with personal upheavals and big choices, we are deciding whom we will become.

Recall the process of "convening" in chapter 8. It contrasts *the expert* with *shared expertise*. The expert sizes things up and tells people what to do. Shared expertise combines local knowledge and outside knowledge by sharing data, success stories, and simplifying models. The goal here is to kindle creative problem-solving by locals. Originally developed as a tool for helping countries, convening is also a useful construct for how we should share and serve others, say as counselors, friends, and family members.

We also raised the possibility that a process like convening can help us help ourselves. When we face an upheaval or have to make a transformative decision, we can consider data, success stories, and simplifying models. Here are the corresponding steps:

1. What's the problem? The challenges: where we stand now and in the past. Compared to others: our advantages as well as problems. Use data to characterize and locate the challenges and the alternatives.

2. Where are the heroes? How have others handled these challenges more or less successfully? What can we learn from them about goals, alternatives, implementation, false starts and responses, leadership (including of the self), partnerships, and timing? We might seek exemplars at three levels: behavioral models, role models, and heroes in the grander domains of history, literature, and religion.

3. What's the model? How can an abstraction or checklist help us reframe our choice? How might it guide us to reconsider our goals and alternatives?

18. Maslow, *Religions, Values, and Peak-Experiences*, 56–67.

Notice how our work on heroes applies to both steps 2 and 3. As we have seen, particular exemplars can guide us and inspire us—this is step 2. And the heroic path is a simple model for step 3: calling, insight, gratitude, and sharing and serving.

Appendix 2 provides a detailed checklist that can help us work through the four steps of that path. The goal is to help ourselves think more creatively and practically about our big choices.

An Example

The philosopher Agnes Callard concludes her 2018 book *Aspiration* with a section on motherhood. Deciding whether to have a baby is a transformative decision. Even though we've had a mother and seen other mothers, it's impossible to anticipate what a family may mean to us in the future.

In an interview, she imagines peering into a crystal ball and seeing herself twenty or more years from now.

> [It] would be like watching a movie about someone who looks like me: she will take pleasures in things I don't now enjoy; she will put great stock in things that are now of little significance to me; she will have knowledge about life generally, and, more specifically, what it is like to live as, say, a mother. I am in no position to assess her life as a success or failure—it is her prerogative to look back at me and think, "How little I knew back then!" What makes big decisions big is that they set into motion changes not only in the outside world, but in ourselves. Becoming a mother means having new desires, feelings, habits, knowledge, and even new decision-procedures.[19]

Callard is right that we can't deduce the right answer to a transformative choice. "But no matter how much we increase our investment at the front end—perfecting our minds with thinking classes, long ruminations, novel-reading, and moral algebra—we cannot spare ourselves the agony of learning by doing."[20]

But I believe heroes can help us shape that learning process. First, the exemplars. Who are the mothers we most admire? How do they inspire us with their big choices and their everyday ones? Second, the framework. Parse their notion of a calling in motherhood and reconsider your own. Look for the big insights that have guided how they parent and how those relate to

---

19. Callard, "Don't Overthink It."
20. Callard, "Don't Overthink It."

your big ahas. And, through their stories and their examples, consider what it means as a parent to share and serve. Feel those stories aesthetically rather than just cognitively.

ON THE AESTHETICS OF LEARNING AND DOING

Aesthetically? That last sentence opens a larger topic relevant to heroes in our lives: how we learn from heroism and how we put their examples into action.

If there were an abstract to this book, it might read:

> A full human life is personified by the hero, and it lies far away from withdrawal or greed. Across many cultures and walks of life, many heroes follow a stylized path. They are buffeted by upheavals in society and in themselves. They must make transformative decisions. They receive or discover a calling. They obtain a big insight. In gratitude and with compassion, they share the calling and insight and serve. And even though we are ordinary people, their heroic examples can help us deal with our upheavals and their stylized path can inspire our own callings, insights, and service.

Got it? Are you sure? What can be captured or conveyed through these, or any, summary sentences? What is someone to do with any argument that comes in a sealed container, with or without preservatives?

Søren Kierkegaard said you could never *derive* an answer to a transformative decision, at least not in the sense of a logical proof or a statistical finding. Modern philosophy, he lamented, "has a comical presupposition, occasioned by its having forgotten, in a sort of world-historical absentmindedness, what it means to be a human being . . . what it means that you and I and he are human beings, each one for himself."[21] Traditions are fine, he said, but they can't help us with the essence of our big choices: "[T]hat which is genuinely human no generation learns from the foregoing . . . Thus no generation has learned from another to love, no generation begins at any other point than the beginning, no generation has a shorter task assigned to it than had the preceding generation . . . But the highest passion in a man is faith, and here no generation begins at any other point than did the preceding generation, every generation begins all over again."[22]

---

21. Kierkegaard, *Concluding Unscientific Postscript*, 109.

22. Kierkegaard, *Fear and Trembling*, 130.

Kierkegaard attacked the philosopher Georg Hegel, whom Kierkeg-aard characterized as trying to deduce from general principles what good and bad are, and therefore what a good human life is. Kierkegaard replied, "No way" (my translation). You cannot sit down and deduce whom to be-come, he said. You cannot derive the purpose and meaning of your indi-vidual existence from someone's book.

But wait: Kierkegaard wrote books. What did he think he was doing? His tomes have titles like *Fear and Trembling, Concluding Unscientific Post-script*, and *Purity of Heart Is to Will One Thing*. Surely, he wrote with the goal that his readers would *get it*: learn something about a full human life, receive some guidance about existential choices.

Kierkegaard's arguments were not statistical. They were not deductive. His means and metaphors were rhetorical (in the original lofty sense of that word) and artistic; they involved "unscientific" leaps of faith. We may "get it" through exemplars in life and in art. (Which recalls a line from a man about as different from Kierkegaard as possible, Oscar Wilde, who chirped: "One should either be a work of art, or wear a work of art.")[23] Heroes inspire us, in literature and legend, history and religion, and also in the real world around us, because their lives are works of art that matter to us.

What is the antithesis of a work of art? Many things, I'm sure, but let me highlight one category: the cliché, the adage, the recipe. Big insights are poorly conveyed by maxims, as Thomas Macaulay noted long ago:

> Every man who has seen the world knows that nothing is so use-less as a general maxim. If it be very moral and very true, it may serve for a copy to a charity-boy. If, like those of Rochefoucault, it be sparkling and whimsical, it may make an excellent motto for an essay. But few indeed of the many wise apophthegms which have been uttered, from the time of the Seven Sages to that of Poor Richard, have prevented a single foolish action.[24]

In Thornton Wilder's novel *The Bridge of San Luis Rey*, Brother Juniper investigates the lives of the people who happened to perish when the bridge collapsed.[25] Brother Juniper reasons that their deaths could not have been random. A scientific study by him of the common characteristics of the victims will, he thinks with delight, provide evidence of God's existence to skeptics of his faith. Alas, we discover along the way that Brother Juniper's enterprise is not appreciated by his superiors. To them, his quest for "evi-dence" is itself heretical, and they burn him at the stake.

23. Wilde, *Complete Works*, 177.

24. Macaulay, *Poetry and Prose*, 263.

25. Wilder, *Bridge of San Luis Rey*.

The novelist relates that Brother Juniper receives this punishment without understanding it, but having faith that somehow both his quest and his death are also God's will. The stories the imaginary Brother Juniper uncovers are the grist of the novelist's book, which the reader recognizes as a great work of art, with Brother Juniper as a hidden coauthor. Thus, Brother Juniper's fictitious fate inside a work of fiction layers another inspiring complexity on the stories of the various victims, as we readers try to figure out, or feel, what the characters have in common, and what if anything that may signify. We may conclude that in these domains only artistic insight is meaningful.

A heroic life is rarely discovered or conveyed through a recipe or a plan. It may be imagined or experienced through art, or by being (or trying to be) yourself a work of art. Recall a conclusion of chapter 9 on romance and intimacy: "It is the purity of our effort in love that matters, not our prowess or the radius of our talents and influence. When we receive the gift of love, we feel deep down that it is all right for us to be imperfect, all right to be human beings, all right to be confused about what to do and how." So too with how you face your upheavals, make big choices, and tentatively progress down your own heroic path. If you are trying is pure, this may itself be sufficient for artistic and therefore human success; let us leave that as a point for reflection.

We should share and serve, not just in the abstract or for a cause, but through and because of relationships such as friendships and communities, marriage and family. In its ultimate form, heroic serving is an act of love, which changes those who receive it and those who give it. In Ernest Hemingway's *A Farewell to Arms*, the priest comes to see the wounded Lieutenant Henry. Their conversation turns philosophical. The priest says he loves God, and Henry says he understands.

> He looked at me and smiled.
> "You understand but do not love God." "No."
> "You do not love Him at all?" he asked.
> "I am afraid of Him in the night sometimes." "You should love Him."
> "I don't love much."
> "Yes," he said. "You do. What you tell me about in the nights. That is not love. That is only passion and lust. When you love you wish to do things for. You wish to sacrifice for. You wish to serve."[26]

26. The conversation continued: "I don't love." "You will. I know you will. Then you will be happy." "I'm happy. I've always been happy." "It is another thing. You cannot know about it unless you have it." Hemingway, *Farewell to Arms*, 72.

Heroism in the Small

Heroism shows up in the interstices of life. One section of St. Josemaría Escrivá's book *The Way* is entitled "Little Things." Here are two of his observations:

823   Have you noticed how human love consists of little things? Well, divine love also consists of little things.

813   Do everything for love. In that way there will be no little things: everything will be big. Perseverance in the little things for love is heroism.[27]

Opus Dei, which Escrivá founded, carries forward this emphasis on holiness in small things. The organization's one-sentence "Message" declares, "Work, family life, and the ordinary events of each day are opportunities for drawing close to Christ, and making Him known to others."[28]

One finds similar ideas in Mahayana Buddhism. Their human heroes, the bodhisattvas, devote themselves to the service of others. "Liberating or saving those who were lost or suffering becomes the sole life purpose of those who take this Bodhisattva vow, even today."[29] Before departing from the world, the Buddha declared that everyone, including women, could become enlightened, not just monks. Especially in Mahayana Buddhism, enlightenment goes beyond the individual ascetic in solitary seeking; it includes, indeed emphasizes, sharing and serving. "It might be said," writes Charley Linden Thorp, "that for a long period of time monks remained cloistered hearing the Dharma, while the laity were actively working as Bodhisattvas in daily life."[30] Like the bodhisattvas, we can aspire to bring our calling, our insights, and our compassionate desire to share and serve into every little thing we do.

THE CYCLE

New upheavals outside us can become upheavals inside us. New momentous decisions arise. They may throw us off our seemingly solid calling, may crack open our satisfying insight. Burnout happens—on the job, say, but also, alas, in our romantic relationships and in our families. And in extreme cases, our perfect hero may look like a perfect fool (h/t Jackson Browne).

27. Escrivá, *Way*.
28. Opus Dei, "Message."
29. Thorp, "Mahayana Buddhism."
30. Thorp, "Mahayana Buddhism."

Are we back at the start? Not quite. We have learned (we hope)—and learned how to learn. If you speak two languages, the third one is easier to master. Since the last time we faced upheaval and transformative decisions, we know about more heroes and have been more aware of heroic acts. We have more experience with *both/and*; we have developed the maturity of mind to inhabit the tentative. We are aware of multiple callings and perhaps of how to experiment with them. Aware of multiple insights and how to shift between them, link them, merge them perhaps. Aware of a variety of ways to share and serve, from big choices like career lines to our everyday efforts to be heroic in small ways. We have realized that "perseverance in the little things for love is heroism."

Faced with new upheavals and feeling once again lost, but this time let down by what we felt and believed and did with our lives, once again we may feel tempted just to bail, or instead to flail. But we resist hiding and fleeing; perhaps like Erik Erikson, we might say that our "primary interest in the flux of phenomena precluded any attempt to find safety in orthodoxy or escape in heresy."[31] Because we now recognize bailing and flailing in others, we may be able to avoid them ourselves. Jesus Estanislao described it this way:

> Between a mystic/monk who flees from the world with its mess and temptations, and the addict who simply wallows in the pleasures that mess and those temptations offer, there must be a middle ground. That middle ground is taken up by "saints in the middle of the world": they do not flee from the realities of the world but stay immersed in them, yet they refuse to be swallowed up by the realities of the world they are in.[32]

And so, we resolve again to prevail. We face up to our new realities. We put together data on our new situation, on what alternatives are available, and on our aptitudes and interests. We seek out others who have succeeded in situations and choices like ours. We return to texts and rituals and places that before inspired us—and look for new ones.

We commence again our search for behavioral models and role models in the small and for heroes in the large. As we do, what might we say about the kind of hero we should be seeking? A "saint of the middle of the road" who has not withdrawn from the world and its dangers, but is fully engaged in it?[33] And more?

31. Erikson, "Autobiographic Notes," 751.

32. Personal communication, August 17, 2021.

33. I cannot resist inserting here Nietzsche's contrast between two kinds of philosophers, one removed from the world, the other fully engaged: "In fact, the philosopher

Your Life, Your Hero

For you, what would be the characteristics of particularly promising heroes? Given all that we have considered so far, let us conclude this book with some suggestions.

The heroes would have received and would themselves issue a calling. Their calling would resonate with you. Ideally, the calling would speak to you in your unique situation, *and* you would recognize the calling as embracing others, equally unique.

The heroes would have received insights that you can in turn receive through them, so to speak, aesthetically, and especially through their lives as works of art. The heroes' upheavals and big decisions would inspire you as you face your own. The heroes' messages would help you with challenges in the large and in the small.

You might receive from them a calling that feels something like falling in love and a big insight that makes you say "aha!"

Like many deep insights, the insights you gain from these heroes might appear obvious once you have them but paradoxical to those who don't have them. You would also find that there are processes for conveying the insight with some but not complete success—not everyone gets it, even when they try. But the insight itself would not exclude anyone from possessing it. The insight is not equal to a formula or maxim, even if you might later use a formula to remind yourself.

The heroes would share their callings and insights with people like you and me specifically, as individuals. The way they serve, the why of their sacrifice, would exemplify love.

Finally, your ideal heroes would confront inside their lives a contradiction or dilemma that also inhabits the world outside. The grander the dilemmas, and the more you recognize them and empathize with them and are astonished by them, the greater the hero's resonance and relevance will be.

---

has long been mistaken and confused by the multitude, either with the scientific man and ideal scholar, or with the religiously elevated, desensualized, desecularized visionary and God-intoxicated man; and even yet when one hears anybody praised, because he lives 'wisely,' or 'as a philosopher,' it hardly means anything more than 'prudently and apart.' Wisdom: that seems to the populace to be a kind of flight, a means and artifice for withdrawing successfully from a bad game; but the GENUINE philosopher—does it not seem so to US, my friends?—lives 'unphilosophically' and 'unwisely,' above all, IMPRUDENTLY, and feels the obligation and burden of a hundred attempts and temptations of life—he risks HIMSELF constantly, he plays THIS bad game." Nietzsche, *Beyond Good and Evil*, §205.

Acknowledgments

First and foremost, and as always, I am grateful to Elaine van Biljon Klitgaard for her insight, encouragement, and example. Elaine epitomizes a full human life. To me and many others, she is a hero.

Thanks to Claremont Graduate University for providing a sabbatical in the second half of 2021, during which this book was completed. Elaine and I spent this time in Bhutan, and we are grateful for their friendship and support to His Majesty Jigme Khesar Namgyel Wangchuck, King of Bhutan; Prime Minister Dr. Lotay Tshering; Director General Dorji Dradhul and the Tourism Council of Bhutan; and especially Director Chewang Rinzin and his team at the Royal Institute for Governance and Strategic Studies.

Kind colleagues have made suggestions on various parts and iterations of this work, leading to many improvements but perhaps not as many as they hoped: Frances Cairncross, Ian Clark, Teresita Cruz-del Rosario, Robert Coulam, Genevéve Fyvie Crysdale, Shalan Crysdale, Jeff Davenport, Donn Dirckx, Jesus P. Estanislao, Johannes W. Fedderke, Garry L. Hagberg, Theresa Hecht, Greg Hughes, Jeannette R. Ickovics, Kevin M. Iga, Ira A. Jackson, Thomas Glenn Jackson III, Kristen N. Klitgaard, Thomas J. Klitgaard, William E. Klitgaard, Tommy Koh, Katherine Marshall, John J. McDermott III, Kimberly June Miller, Ellen Palevsky, Mashi Rahmani, Dennis A. Romig, Laurie Romig, Becca Rothfeld, Vijay Sathe, Thomas C. Schelling, Michael S. Segal, Robert A. Skotheim, Benjamin Smith, Carl H. Taylor, Tyler Thorpe, Robert E. Wycoff, Richard J. Zeckhauser, and Ivan Zupan.

The usual caveat protecting these courteous people from further responsibility is, of course, in order.

Three chapters draw on earlier publications:

Chapters 2–3: "Hermits, Addicts, and Heroes." *International Journal of Religion and Spirituality in Society* 10:1 (2020) 29–40.

Chapter 6: "From Insight to Ideology." *Theoria: A Journal of Social and Political Theory* 83/84 (1994) 167–79.

Chapter 9: "On Romance and Intimacy." *Philosophy and Literature* 43:2 (2019) 482–500.

Appendix 1

Discussion Questions

The book is organized into four sections and eleven chapters. My favorite discussion prompt for any chapter, section, or book is this: "Bring along a passage you especially like and be prepared to explain why."

The questions below are not exhaustive, nor should they be exhausting; discussion leaders can choose among them depending on the interests, backgrounds, and time budgets of the group.

PART I: BAIL, FLAIL, OR PREVAIL

Chapter 1. Upheavals and Big Decisions

1. The chapter gives examples of upheavals in people's lives. What examples have you seen or experienced?

2. Have you been through something like burnout? If so, describe how it felt and what it did to your ability to think clearly about next steps.

3. "Transformative decisions" are big, life-altering choices such as what to study and what careers to try, moving across the country or around the world, embracing or leaving a community of faith, getting married, starting a family, and more. They have in common great uncertainty about the future and the fact that these choices will determine in some sense whom we become. What is an example of a transformative decision you have experienced?

Chapter 2. Ascetics and Addicts

1. Give an example of someone confronting turbulence in their lives by "bailing" on things.

2. What examples have you seen of "flailing," where people respond to upheaval by abandoning things that guided them and restrained them in the past?

3. What do you think of the argument that ascetics and addicts both experience a kind of living death?

4. Have you ever felt a scorn like Nietzsche's against the person who makes a life goal of "getting a good night's sleep"?

Chapter 3. Heroes

1. Name a hero of history or literature who has mattered to you. What is it about their story that resonates with you?

2. What do you think of the idea of "everyday heroes"? Know any? Why are they admirable?

Chapter 4. For Non-Heroes Too?

1. Do you know anyone who has said, "I just want to be average"? What were the circumstances?

2. What do you think of the idea of a training program for everyday heroes?

3. How do you think we can learn from and be inspired by heroes, even though we may feel anything but heroic ourselves?

PART II: PREPARING TO PREVAIL

Chapter 5. Calling, or Purpose

1. Do you know someone who has always seemed to know their calling or purpose in life? (Are you one of them?)

2. Moritz Schlick said that we'll be happiest when we do things for their own sake, as when we play. What do you think of his argument?

3. The chapter presents five categories of calling. Have any of them been paramount in your life? Which of them seems most in line with you now?

4. If someone isn't sure of their calling but has several candidates, how would you advise them to experiment?

Chapter 6. Big Insights

1. An insight gives a feeling of "aha!" What's an example that you've experienced where a puzzle you confronted was suddenly resolved?

2. The chapter examines four big insights, which are "cognitive models or theories that suddenly make sense of a series of puzzles in our world, perhaps also in ourselves." The four were the economic insight, the Marxist insight, the Protestant insight, and the process insight. Have you experienced any of these four in action?

3. How can a helpful insight degenerate into a pernicious ideology? Have you seen this happen?

4. The author received a couple of big insights from Frederick Mosteller. What were they? Do they ring true in your experience?

Chapter 7. Gratitude

1. Share examples of something big and something small that you're grateful for.

2. Consider William James's argument that our behaviors shape our attitudes. Can you think of an example in your life?

3. "Gratitude is virtue in the receiver, and a key to this virtue is simply being *aware*." What does this mean to you?

Chapter 8. Share and Serve

1. Give an example where you were the recipient of "sharing and serving" but it didn't work. What was it about the experience that put you off?

2. In the discussion of international development, what are the author's two approaches to expertise? How have you experienced something like them in your life?

3. How might the process of "convening" be useful to us in confronting personal upheavals and making transformative decisions?

4. What do you think of John Steinbeck's argument that in some ways receiving well is more valuable than giving well?

PART III: HEROES CLOSE TO HOME

Chapter 9. Romance and Intimacy

1. In your experience, how well do you think philosophers and theologians handle the topic of romance and intimacy? Explain.

2. Which of this chapter's examples of great romance did you like most, and why?

3. "The jolt and surprise of romantic love, its physicality and yet its transporting otherworldliness, its radical *unselfing*, are signs and metaphors for meaning in life." Discuss.

4. How do you think a couple might try to follow the hero's path together and develop mutual callings, insight, gratitude, and ways to share and serve?

PART IV: RECURRENCE

Chapter 10. Backsliding

1. Have you seen or experienced backsliding in your life? Please share.

2. Give two examples of ways people prevent backsliding. Have you used any of these tricks and tools yourself?

3. How can ways to prevent backsliding turn into part of the problem?

4. Give an example of how cues can trigger destructive, addictive behavior. How might we instead employ positive cues to trigger our best selves?

Chapter 11. Your Flourishing Life

1. What does it mean to say that a heroic life can best be communicated through art and example rather than science and statistics? Do you agree?

2. To you, what are the characteristics of ideal heroes?

3. What are your personal takeaways from this book? How do they connect with your current challenges and opportunities?

Appendix 2

A Checklist for Facing Upheaval and Making Big Choices

A CONVENING OF YOUR OWN

Recall the discussion of "convening" in chapter 8. This process combines local expertise with outside expertise with the goal of kindling creative problem-solving. When you face a transformative decision, you might think of organizing a convening of your own.

The local expertise is yours—you have unique knowledge of your challenges, goals, opportunities, and constraints. But outside experts can help you by providing data, examples, and models that you may not yet know. For you right now, an outside expert might be a friend, a counselor, a therapist, a religious leader, a teacher, or a specialist who knows a lot about the particular decision that you face. Or a combination of them. You might join others facing your transformative choice, or you might work alone with your expert(s).

And then, with their help, you can work through these three steps:

1. *Data*. What upheavals have happened or threaten you? What are your options? Collect information about them, comparing yourself and your situation with other people's. Using such data to locate your

transformative decision has several benefits. For one thing, you may realize with relief that you're not alone.

2. *Success story.* Identify exemplars and heroes who, facing upheavals and decisions like yours, have succeeded—not in reaching perfection, but by progressing along a dynamic path of improvement. Explore their stories. If you or your outside experts know of real-life heroes of relevance, perhaps invite them to discuss things with you.

3. *Model or framework.* Then you can apply to your situation the steps of calling, insight, gratitude, and sharing and serving (recall figure 2).

Figure 2

The Path to Prevailing

A. CALLING

Related to your decision, what is your calling (purpose)? If you need to realize or rethink your calling, work through chapter 5 and consider these questions:

1. Fulfilling Yourself

What activities matter to you for their own sake? Recall Schlick on play, Csikszentmihalyi on flow, Nietzsche on listing such activities, and reflect on what they have in common.

How might you find various levels of exemplars—adepts in particular activities that seem to you to matter for their own sake (say, woodworking or skateboarding), role models in the broader activity of which that is a part (say, a renowned craftsperson or a champion athlete), and heroes whose calling, big insights, and sharing and serving can inspire you to rethink your own journey?

2. Fulfilling Others

Consider the altruistic calling. With regard to your choices now and people you're considering, what makes them happy? On the other extreme, what makes them unhappy (not always the opposite of what makes them happy)? At a broader level, what kind of society is likely to exhibit more happiness and less unhappiness, more kindness, less cruelty, more chances for people to fulfill themselves? More heroism in the small and the large?

How might you find various levels of exemplars—people who seem to have made others happy in a particular activity close to your choice, role models (recall moral exemplars, activist heroes, and more), and heroes writ large, including societies you admire—where you study their callings, big insights, and ways of sharing and serving?

3. Science, or Seeking Truth

Which truths matter to you and why? What methods seem to you most likely to uncover truths of various kinds? In these spaces of substance and method, where might your calling lie?

How might you seek out various levels of exemplars—admirable scientists or scholars within a particular subfield of interest to you, role models of the scientific life who seem to have uncovered or debunked truth, and heroes writ large, perhaps outside of science per se, whose calling, big insights, and sharing and serving can inspire you to rethink your own journey?

4. Art, or Creativity Seeking Authenticity

What forms of art inspire you? What artistic activities have for you seemed most fruitful so far? How might you become more involved in consuming art, producing it, curating it, teaching it, and teaching about it? (More than one answer is possible.)

How might you find various levels of exemplars—participants in the artistic life whose specific skills can guide you (a sculptor or museum curator or art teacher), role models of the creative life more broadly, and heroes writ large, perhaps outside of art per se, whose calling, big insights, and sharing and serving can inspire you to rethink your own journey?

5. *Engaging with Ultimate Reality*

What religious or spiritual experiences have inspired you? What were their effects on you, including questions they raised? In your experience, how have various doctrines and practices enhanced or inhibited such experiences? What commonalities exist across various ways to engage with Ultimate Reality?

How might you find various levels of exemplars—adepts in particular activities such as meditation, role models in practicing or leading or sharing faith, and heroes of the faith whose calling, big insights, and sharing and serving can inspire you to rethink your own journey?

Experiments

Finally, if one or more of these callings seems important for your decision, how might you *experiment* with it/them?

B. INSIGHT

Recall the examples in chapter 6 and the typology of big insights presented there. With regard to your transformative decision, what big insights seem most relevant?

Think of ways your big choice is surfacing contradictions inside yourself. Write them down.

Now, look around you. Do you see these contradictions there as well? How might your transformative decision enable you to work on the contradiction in yourself and the contradiction in the world at the same time? (Recall Erikson.)

Seek relevant exemplars. How have other people faced these contradictions and conflicts? Have some of them made a successful transformative decision akin to the one you're facing? How did they do it? Did they have a big insight that helped them overcome their contradictions? Is there a generalization of that insight for you?

If a big insight emerges or is reinforced by your answers, beware of the slide from insight to ideology. With your big insight, how can you maintain a both/and perspective? (Recall Kuhn, Mosteller.) With regard to your big choice, how might you keep more than one big insight in mind?

C. GRATITUDE

Consider the benefits of gratitude and how to promote it in ourselves (chapter 7).

Perhaps many things are in upheaval now, and big uncertainties have created big anxieties. Lots may seem wrong out there in the world at large and in your personal travails as well. Nonetheless, even now, what's going *right*?

What was right before the upheaval? What can you learn from that?

Think of a time when you experienced something like grace—the feeling of a gift coming from outside yourself, perhaps unbidden and perhaps undeserved. Recall the details. How might you cue that feeling of grace again? (Recall chapter 10 on backsliding.)

D. SHARE AND SERVE

Revisit chapter 8. Then consider carefully this big and complicated question: How can you right now "get over yourself" and find ways to share and serve through your example—especially in the little things you do, almost like small works of art?

Bibliography

Acampora, Lauren. "Véra Nabokov: Vladimir Nabokov's Wife." In *The Who, the What, and the When*, edited by Jenny Volvovksi, Julia Rothman, and Matt Lamothe, 16–17. San Francisco: Chronicle Books, 2014.

Acocella, Joan. "Renaissance Man: A New Translation of Boccaccio's Decameron." *The New Yorker*, November 11, 2013. https://www.newyorker.com/magazine/2013/11/11/renaissance-man-4.

Aella. "How I Lost My Faith." *Knowingless* (blog), April 24, 2017. https://knowingless.com/2017/04/24/how-i-lost-my-faith/.

———. "10 Months of Acid." *Knowingless* (blog), August 21, 2016. https://knowingless.com/2016/08/21/421/.

Agassi, Joseph. "Genius in Science." *Philosophy of the Social Sciences* 5:2 (1975) 145–61.

Allen, Summer. *The Science of Awe*. Berkeley: Greater Good Science Center, University of California, 2018. https://www.templeton.org/wp-content/uploads/2018/08/White-Paper_Awe_FINAL.pdf.

Allison, Scott T., and George R. Goethals. *Heroes: Who They Are and What They Do*. Oxford: Oxford University Press, 2011.

———. *Heroic Leadership: An Influence Taxonomy of 100 Exceptional Individuals*. London: Routledge, 2013.

Arpin-Ricci, Jamie. "Preach the Gospel at All Times?" *HuffPost*, July 1, 2012. https://www.huffpost.com/entry/preach-the-gospel-at-all-times-st-francis_b_1627781.

Bernheim, B. Douglas, and Antonio Rangel. "Addiction and Cue-Triggered Decision Processes." *American Economic Review* 94:5 (2004) 1558–90.

Bierce, Ambrose. *The Devil's Dictionary*. Oxford: Oxford University Press, 1999. First published 1906.

Boccaccio, Giovanni. *The Decameron*. Translated by Wayne A. Rebhorn. New York: Norton, 2013. First published 1353.

Bornstein, David. *How to Change the World: Social Entrepreneurs and the Power of New Ideas*. Oxford: Oxford University Press, 2004.

Boyd, Brian. "Envelopes for the Letters to Véra." In *Letters to Véra*, translated and edited by Olga Veronina and Brian Boyd, xix–xlix. New York: Knopf Borzoi, 2014.

Bradley, A.C. *Shakespearean Tragedy: Lectures on Hamlet, Othello, King Lear, Macbeth*. London: Macmillan, 1904.

Brinton, Crane. *Nietzsche*. Cambridge: Harvard University Press, 1941.

Bronk, Kendall Cotton. "The Exemplar Methodology: An Approach to Studying the Leading Edge of Development." *Psychological Well-Being: Theory, Research and Practice* 2:5 (2012) 1–10.

Bronk, Kendall Cotton, et al. "Claremont Purpose Scale: A Measure that Assesses the Three Dimensions of Purpose among Adolescents." *Research in Human Development* 15:1 (2018) 1–17.

Bronk, Kendall Cotton, and Caleb Mitchell. "Youth Purpose: A Translational Research Agenda." In *The Ecology of Purposeful Living across the Lifespan: Developmental, Educational, and Social Perspectives*, edited by Anthony L. Burrow and Patrick L. Hill, 233–48. Cham, Switzerland: Springer Nature, 2020.

Brunner, Emil. *Our Faith.* Translated by John W. Rilling. New York: Scribner, 1962. First published 1936.

Callard, Agnes. *Aspiration: The Agency of Becoming.* Oxford: Oxford University Press, 2018.

———. "Don't Overthink It." *Boston Review*, 21 January 2019. http://bostonreview.net/ philosophy-religion/agnes-callard-dont-overthink-it.

Campbell, Joseph. *The Hero with a Thousand Faces.* 3rd ed. The Collected Works of Joseph Campbell. Bollingen Series 17. Joseph Campbell Foundation. Novato, CA: New World Library, 2008. First published 1949 by Princeton University Press.

———. "The Hero with a Thousand Faces." Interview with Bill Moyers. Excerpt from *Joseph Campbell and the Power of Myth*, episode 1, n.d. https://youtu.be/Byli-Y8KonY.

Carroll, Raymonde. *Cultural Misunderstandings: The French-American Experience.* Chicago: University of Chicago Press, 1988.

Cavell, Stanley. *Must We Mean What We Say?: A Book of Essays.* Updated ed. Cambridge: Cambridge University Press, 2002. First published 1969 by Scribner.

Chesterton, G. K. *Saint Francis of Assisi.* London: Hodder and Stoughton, 1924.

Cohen, Josh. *Not Working: Why We Have to Stop.* London: Granta: 2019.

Cohen, Josh. "The Best Books on Burnout." Interview with Cal Flyn. *Five Books* (blog), n.d. https://fivebooks.com/best-books/burnout-work-exhaustion-josh-cohen/.

Colby, Anne, and William Damon. *Some Do Care: Contemporary Lives of Moral Commitment.* New York: Free Press, 1992.

Collingwood, R. G. *An Autobiography.* Oxford: Oxford University Press, 1939.

Cuddihy, John Murray. *The Ordeal of Civility: Freud, Marx, Lévi-Strauss and the Jewish Struggle with Modernity.* 2nd ed. Boston: Beacon, 1987. First published 1974.

Curtius, Ernst Robert. *European Literature and the Late Middle Ages.* Translated by Willard R. Trask. Bollingen Series 36. Princeton, NJ: Princeton University Press, 1953. First published 1948.

Csikszentmihalyi, Mihaly. *Flow: The Psychology of Optimal Experience.* New York: HarperCollins, 2008. First published 1990.

Dahl, Robert A. *After the Revolution?: Authority in a Good Society.* Rev. ed. New Haven, CT: Yale University Press, 1990. First published 1970.

Deal, Terrence E., and Allan A. Kennedy. *Corporate Cultures: The Rites and Rituals of Corporate Life*, Rev. ed. New York: Basic Books, 2000. First published 1980.

Dickens, Leah R. "Using Gratitude to Promote a Positive Change: A Series of Meta-Analyses Investigating the Effectiveness of Gratitude Interventions." *Basic and Applied Social Psychology* 39:4 (2017) 193–208.

Dik, Bryan J., et al. "Career Callings and Career Development." In *International Handbook of Career Guidance*, 2nd ed., edited by James A. Athanasou and Harsha N. Perera, 185–206. Geneva: Springer, 2020.

Dik, Bryan J., and Ryan Duffy. *Make Your Job a Calling: How the Psychology of Vocation Can Change Your Life at Work*. West Conshohocken, PA: Templeton, 2012.

Dillard, Annie. *An American Childhood*. New York: Harper & Row, 1987.

———. *The Maytrees*. New York: HarperCollins, 2007.

———. *Three by Annie Dillard*. New York: Perennial, 2001.

Easterly, William. *The Tyranny of Experts: Economists, Dictators, and the Forgotten Rights of the Poor*. New York: Basic Books, 2014.

Emmons, Robert. *Thanks!: How the New Science of Gratitude Can Make You Happier*. New York: Houghton Mifflin, 2007.

Erikson, Erik H. "Autobiographic Notes on the Identity Crisis." *Daedalus* 99:4 (1970) 730–59.

———. *Gandhi's Truth: On the Origins of Militant Nonviolence*. New York: Norton, 1994. First published 1969.

———. *Young Man Luther: A Study in Psychoanalysis and History*. New York: Norton, 1958.

Floyd, Simeon, et al. "Research Article: Universals and Cultural Diversity in the Expression of Gratitude." *Royal Society Open Science* 5:180391 (2018) 1–9. doi: 10.1098/rsos.180391.

Folbigg, Zoë. "A Commuter Romance." *Outlook*, BBC World Service, November 2, 2017. https://www.bbc.co.uk/programmes/p05lvl77.

———. *The Note*. London: Aria, 2017.

Franco, Zeno E., et al. "Heroism Research: A Review of Theories, Methods, Challenges, and Trends." *Journal of Humanistic Psychology* 58:4 (2018) 382–96.

Freudenberger, Nell. *The Newlyweds*. New York: Knopf, 2012.

Frisk, Kristian. "What Makes a Hero? Theorising the Social Structuring of Heroism." *Sociology*. 53:1 (2019) 87–103.

Fukuyama, Francis. *Identity: The Demand for Dignity and the Politics of Resentment*. New York: Farrar, Straus and Giroux, 2018.

Ganzevoort, Reinder Ruard. "Crisis Experiences and the Development of Belief and Unbelief." In *Belief and Unbelief: Psychological Perspectives*, edited by Jozef Corveleyn and Dirk Hutsebaut, 21–38. Amsterdam: Editions Rodopi BV, 1994.

Geertz, Clifford. "'From the Native's Point of View': On the Nature of Anthropological Understanding." In *Culture Theory: Essays on Mind, Self, and Emotion*, edited by Richard A. Shweder and Robert A. LeVine, 26–45. Cambridge: Cambridge University Press, 1984.

Gibson, Donald E. "Role Models." In *Encyclopedia of Career Development*, edited by Jeffrey H. Greenhaus and Gerard A. Callanan, 701–3. Thousand Oaks, CA: Sage, 2006.

Gladwell, Malcolm. *Outliers: The Story of Success*. New York: Little, Brown, 2008.

Goethe, Johann Wolfgang von. *Wilhelm Meister's Apprenticeship and Travels*. Translated by Thomas Carlyle. 2nd ed. London: Chapman and Hall, 1874. First published 1795.

Heath, Chip, and Dan Heath. *Switch: How to Change Things When Change Is Hard*. New York: Broadway, 2010.

Hemingway, Ernest. *A Farewell to Arms*. New York: Scribner, 1995. First published 1929.

Hesse, Hermann. *The Glass Bead Game (Magister Ludi)*. Translated by Richard Winston and Clara Winston. New York: Holt, Rinehart and Winston, 1969. First published 1943.

Holmes, Richard. *The Age of Wonder: The Romantic Generation and the Discovery of the Beauty and Terror of Science*. New York: Pantheon, 2008.

Hook, Sidney. *The Hero in History: A Study in Limitation and Possibility*. Boston: Beacon, 1955. First published 1943.

Horner, Avril, and Anne Rowe. "Introduction." In *Living on Paper: Letters from Iris Murdoch, 1934–1995*, edited by Avril Horner and Anne Rowe, xi–xx. Princeton, NJ: Princeton University Press, 2016.

Huysmans, Joris-Karl. *Against the Grain (À Rebours)*. Translated by John Howard. Vancouver: Royal Classics, 2021. First published 1884. Project Gutenberg ebook. https://www.gutenberg.org/files/12341/12341-h/12341-h.

Hyde, Lewis. *The Gift: Creativity and the Artist in the Modern World*. New York: Vintage, 2007. First published 1983.

———. *Trickster Makes This World: Mischief, Myth, and Art*. New York: Farrar, Straus and Giroux, 2010. First published 1998.

"Imitation of Christ." In *The Catholic Encyclopedia*, vol. 7. New York: Appleton, 1910. http://www.newadvent.org/cathen/07674c.htm.

"Inaugural Address of President Benigno S. Aquino III (English Translation)." *Official Gazette*, June 30, 2010. https://www.officialgazette.gov.ph/2010/06/30/inaugural-address-of-president-benigno-s-aquino-iii-english-translation/.

James, William. "The Gospel of Relaxation." In *Talks to Teachers on Psychology: And to Students on Some of Life's Ideals*. New York: Henry Holt, 1925. First published 1899. Project Gutenberg ebook. https://www.gutenberg.org/ebooks/16287.

———. *The Varieties of Religious Experience*. New York: Longmans, Green, 1917. First published 1902. Project Gutenberg ebook. https://www.gutenberg.org/files/621/621-h/621-h.html.

Johnson, Paul. *Heroes: From Alexander the Great and Julius Caesar to Churchill and De Gaulle*. New York: Harper, 2007.

Jong, Erica. *Fear of Flying*. New York: Henry Holt, 1973.

Juliani, Michael. "Lisa Wells: Tapering of Extremes." *Guernica: A Magazine of Global Arts and Politics*, May 22, 2018. https://www.guernicamag.com/lisa-wells-tapering-of-extremes/.

Jung, Carl G. *The Development of Personality*. Translated by Gerhard Adler and R. F. C. Hull. The Collected Works of C.G. Jung 17. Princeton, NJ: Princeton University Press, 1955. First published 1910.

Kant, Immanuel. *The Metaphysics of Morals*. Translated by Mary Gregor. Cambridge: Cambridge University Press, 1996. First published 1785.

Kempis, Thomas à. *The Imitation of Christ*. Translated by Leo Sherley-Price. London: Penguin, 1952. First published 1441.

Kierkegaard, Søren. *Concluding Unscientific Postscript*. Translated by David F. Swenson and Walter Lowrie. Princeton, NJ: Princeton University Press for American-Scandinavian Foundation, 1941. First published 1846.

———. *Fear and Trembling*. Translated by Walter Lowrie. New York: Anchor, 1954. First published 1843.

———. *The Sickness unto Death*. Translated by Walter Lowrie. New York: Anchor, 1954. First published 1849.

Kinsella, Elaine Louise, et al. "Zeroing in on Heroes: A Prototype Analysis of Hero Features." *Journal of Personality and Social Psychology* 108:1 (2015) 114–27.

Klitgaard, Robert. *Adjusting to Reality: Beyond "State vs. Market" in Economic Development*. London: Routledge, 2021. First published 1991 by Institute for Contemporary Studies Press.

———. *The Culture and Development Manifesto*. Oxford: Oxford University Press, 2021.

———. "Engaging Corruption: New Ideas for the International Monetary Fund." *Policy Design and Practice* 2:3 (2019) 229–42.

Koestler, Arthur. *The Act of Creation*. New York: Macmillan, 1964.

Kuhn, Thomas S. *The Essential Tension: Selected Studies in Scientific Tradition and Change*. Chicago: University of Chicago Press, 1977.

———. *The Structure of Scientific Revolutions*. Chicago: University of Chicago Press, 1962.

Langer, Suzanne K. *Philosophy in a New Key: A Study in the Symbolism of Reason, Rite, and Art*. 3rd ed. Cambridge, MA: Harvard University Press, 1957.

LeCompte, Rowan. Interview with Scott Simon. National Public Radio, April 11, 2009. http://www.npr.org/templates/player/mediaPlayer.html?action=1&t=1&islist=false&id=102977788&m=102997707.

Levitsky, Steven, and Daniel Ziblatt. *How Democracies Die*. New York: Broadway, 2018.

"Life-Changing Epiphany Wears Off on Ride Home." *The Onion*, November 5, 2014. https://local.theonion.com/life-changing-epiphany-wears-off-on-ride-home-1819577152.

Little, Brian R. *Me, Myself, and Us: The Science of Personality and the Art of Well-Being*. New York: Public Affairs, 2014.

Lonergan, Bernard. *Insight: A Study of Human Understanding*. Edited by Frederick E. Crowe and Robert M. Doran. 5th ed. Collected Works of Bernard Lonergan 3. Toronto: University of Toronto Press, 1992. First published 1957 by Longmans, Green.

Luther, Martin. "Concerning Christian Liberty." Translated by R. S. Grignon. *Harvard Classics*, Vol. 36, part 6, pp. 339–65. New York: Collier, 1938. First published 1520.

Macaulay, Thomas Babington. *Macaulay: Poetry and Prose*. Edited by G. M. Young. Cambridge: MA, Harvard University Press, 1967. First published 1827.

Mandeville, Bernard. *The Fable of the Bees and Other Writings*. Edited by E. J. Hundert. Indianapolis: Hackett, 1987. First published 1714.

Marcet, Albert, and Juan P. Nicolini. "Recurrent Hyperinflations and Learning." *American Economic Review* 9:5 (2003) 1476–98.

Martela, Frank, and Michael F. Steger. "The Three Meanings of Meaning in Life: Distinguishing Coherence, Purpose, and Significance." *Journal of Positive Psychology* 11:5 (2016) 531–45.

Maslach, Christina. "Burned-Out." *Human Behavior* 5:9 (1976) 16–22.

Maslow, Abraham H. *The Farther Reaches of Human Nature*. New York: Viking, 1971.

———. *Religions, Values, and Peak-Experiences*. Columbus: Ohio State University Press, 1964

———. *Toward a Psychology of Being*. New York: Van Nostrand, 1962.

Matthews, Steve. "Chronic Automaticity in Addiction: Why Extreme Addiction Is a Disorder." *Neuroethics* 10:1 (2017) 199–209.

Maugham, W. Somerset. *The Razor's Edge*. Philadelphia: Blakiston, 1944.

Mauss, Marcel. *The Gift: The Form and Reason for Exchange in Archaic Societies.* Translated by W. D. Halls. New York: Norton, 1990. First published 1925.

Mawson, T. J. *God and the Meanings of Life: What God Could and Couldn't Do to Make Our Lives More Meaningful.* London: Bloomsbury, 2016.

McClelland, David C. et al., *The Achievement Motive.* Barakaldo, 2020. Ebook. First published 1953 by Appleton-Century-Crofts.

McClelland, David C. *The Achieving Society.* New York: Irvington, 1976. First published 1961 by Van Nostrand.

Mele, Alfred R. *Backsliding: Understanding Weakness of Will.* Oxford: Oxford University Press, 2012.

Metz, Thaddeus. "The Meaning of Life." In *The Stanford Encyclopedia of Philosophy,* edited by Edward N. Zalta. Summer 2013 ed. https://plato.stanford.edu/archives/sum2013/entries/life-meaning.

Mill, John Stuart. *Autobiography and Literary Essays.* Edited by John M. Robson and Jack Stillinger. Vol. 1 of *Collected Works of John Stuart Mill,* edited by John M. Robson. Oxford: Routledge, 1981.

Monson, Elizabeth, and Chorten Tshering. *More Than a Madman: The Divine Words of Drukpa Kunley.* Thimphu, Bhutan: Institute for Language and Culture Studies, 2014.

Moorhouse, Geoffrey. *Beyond All Reason: Monastic Life in the Twentieth Century.* London: Weidenfeld & Nicolson, 1969.

Morrison, Richard. "Andris Nelsons's Rapid Rise to the Top." *The Times of London,* December 18, 2009. http://entertainment.timesonline.co.uk/tol/arts_and_entertainment/music/classical/article6960663.ece.

Murdoch, Iris. *Metaphysics as a Guide to Morals.* London: Penguin, 1992.

———. *The Sacred and the Profane Love Machine.* New York: Viking, 1974.

———. *The Sovereignty of Good.* Oxford: Routledge Classics, 1970.

Nabokov, Vladimir. *Letters to Véra.* Edited and translated by Olga Veronina and Brian Boyd. New York: Knopf Borzoi, 2014.

Nagy, Gregory. *The Ancient Greek Hero in 24 Hours.* Cambridge, MA: Harvard University Press, 2013.

———. "The Epic Hero." 2nd ed. (online version). Washington, DC: Center for Hellenic Studies, 2005. http://nrs.harvard.edu/urn-3:hlnc.essay:Nagy.The_Epic_Hero.2005.

Nakamura, Jeanne, and Mihaly Csikszentmihalyi. "The Construction of Meaning through Vital Engagement." In *Flourishing: Positive Psychology and the Life Well-Lived,* edited by Corey L. M. Keyes and Jonathan Haidt, 83–104. Washington, DC: American Psychological Association, 2003.

Nelsons, Andris. Interview with Harriet Gilbert. *The Strand,* July 19, 2010. http://www.bbc.co.uk/programmes/p008lmss#p008y24c.

Nhat Hanh, Thich. *Living Buddha, Living Christ.* New York: Riverhead, 1995.

Niebuhr, Reinhold. *The Nature and Destiny of Man: A Christian Interpretation.* Vol. 1. New York: Scribner, 1941.

Nietzsche, Friedrich. *Beyond Good and Evil.* Translated by Helen Zimmern. The Complete Works of Friedrich Nietzsche (1909–1913). Project Gutenberg ebook, 2009. First published 1886. https://www.gutenberg.org/files/4363/4363-h/4363-h.htm.

———. *Ecce Homo.* Translated by Walter Kaufman. In *Basic Writings of Nietzsche,* edited by Walter Kaufman. New York: Modern Library, 1992. First published 1888.

————. *The Gay Science*. Translated by Thomas Common, Paul V. Cohn, and Maude D. Petre. Honolulu: University Press of the Pacific, 2003. First published 1882.

————. *Human, All Too Human: A Book for Free Spirits*. Translated by R. J. Hollingdale. Cambridge: Cambridge University Press, 1996. First published 1878.

————. "Schopenhauer as Educator." In *Thoughts Out of Season, Part II*, by Friedrich Nietzsche, translated by Adrian Collins, 103–201. Edinburgh: T. N. Foulis, 1909. First published 1874. Project Gutenberg ebook. https://www.gutenberg.org/ebooks/38226

————. *Thus Spake Zarathustra: A Book for All and None*. Translated by Thomas Common. New York: Macmillan, 1911. First published 1883.

Noonan, John T., Jr. *Bribes*. New York: Macmillan, 1984.

Nussbaum, Martha. "'Faint with Secret Knowledge': Love and Vision in Murdoch's *The Black Prince*." In *Iris Murdoch: Philosopher*, edited by Justin Broackes, 135–53. Oxford: Oxford University Press, 2012.

Opus Dei. "Message." https://opusdei.org/en/article/message/.

"The Other-Worldly Philosophers." *The Economist*, July 16, 2009. https://www.economist.com/briefing/2009/07/16/the-other-worldly-philosophers.

Otto, Rudolph. *The Idea of the Holy: An Inquiry into the Non-Rational Factor in the Idea of the Divine and Its Relation to the Rational*. Translated by John W. Harvey. Oxford: Oxford University Press, 1958. First published 1923.

Park, Mungo. *The Life and Travels of Mungo Park*. London: John W. Parker, 1838.

Perez, Sarah. "Audible's New Romance Audiobooks Learning to Jump to the Sex Scenes." *TechCrunch*, November 1, 2017. https://techcrunch.com/2017/11/01/audiblesnew-romance-audiobooks-service-uses-machine-learning-to-jump-to-the-sex-scenes/.

Phillips, Bonnie, et al. "Sex Addiction as a Disease: Evidence for Assessment, Diagnosis, and Response to Critics." *Sexual Addiction & Compulsivity: The Journal of Treatment and Prevention* 22 (2015) 167–92.

Pope Francis: A Man of His Word. Netflix, 2018. https://www.imdb.com/title/tt6915100/.

Posner, Richard A. "A Theory of Primitive Society, with Special Reference to Law." *Journal of Law and Economics* 23:1 (1980) 1–53.

Pritchard, Duncan, et al. "Treatment Relapse and Behavioral Momentum Theory." *Journal of Applied Behavior Analysis* 47:4 (2014) 814–33.

Quine, W. V. *From Stimulus to Science*. Cambridge, MA: Harvard University Press, 1995.

Rebhorn, Wayne A. "Introduction." In *The Decameron*, by Giovanni Boccaccio, translated by Wayne A. Rebhorn. New York: Norton, 2013

Ritu, and Madhu Anand. "Gratitude Interventions and Its Applications in Youth." *Indian Journal of Health & Wellbeing* 5:10 (2014) 1232–35.

Robinson, Marilynne. "Credo." *Harvard Divinity Review* 36:2 (2008) 22–27.

Robson, John M., and Jack Stillinger. "Introduction." In *Autobiography and Literary Essays*, edited by John M. Robson and Jack Stillinger. Vol. 1 of *Collected Works of John Stuart Mill*, edited by John M. Robson. Oxford: Routledge, 1981.

Rosaldo, Renato. *Culture and Truth: The Remaking of Social Analysis*. Boston: Beacon, 1989.

Rothfeld, Becca. "Affliction and Salvation." *The Nation*, September 9, 2016. https://www.thenation.com/article/archive/affliction-and-salvation/.

————. "Gone Girl's Feminist Update of the Old-Fashioned Femme Fatale." *The New Republic*, October 9, 2014. https://newrepublic.com/article/119743/gone-girl-has-offered-feminism-new-hero.

Salinger, J. D. *Franny and Zooey*. New York: Little, Brown, 1959.

Sandel, Michael J. "Market Reasoning as Moral Reasoning: Why Economists Should Re-Engage with Political Philosophy." *Journal of Economic Perspectives* 24:4 (2013) 121–40.

Sargeant, Leah Libresco. "Consent and Louis C.K." *First Things*, November 21, 2017. https://www.firstthings.com/web-exclusives/2017/11/consent-and-louis-c-k.

Schechtman, Dan. "Quasi-Crystal, Not Quasi-Scientist." *Frontiers for Young Minds*, September 7, 2021. https://kids.frontiersin.org/articles/10.3389/frym.2020.00022.

Schelling, Thomas C. *Ethics, Law, and the Exercise of Self-Command*. The Tanner Lectures on Human Values. Ann Arbor: University of Michigan, 1982. https://tannerlectures.utah.edu/_documents/a-to-z/s/schelling83.pdf.

———. "The Intimate Contest for Self-Command." *The Public Interest*, 1980, 94–118. https://www.nationalaffairs.com/storage/app/uploads/public/58e/1a4/cd0/58e 1a4cd03a87778521749.pdf.

———. "Self-Command in Practice, in Policy, and in a Theory of Rational Choice." *American Economic Review* 74:2 (1984) 1–11.

Schiff, Stacy. *Véra (Mrs. Vladimir Nabokov)*. New York: Random House, 1999.

Schlick, Moritz. "On the Meaning of Life." In *Philosophical Papers*, vol. 2, *(1925–1936)*, edited by Henk L. Mulder and Barbara F. B. van de Velde-Schlick, translated by Peter Heath, 112–29. Dordrecht: Reidel, 1979. First published 1927.

Schopenhauer, Arthur. *The World as Will and Idea*. Translated by Jill Berman. London: Everyman, 1995. First published 1819.

Segrè, Gino. *Faust in Copenhagen: A Struggle for the Soul of Physics and the Birth of the Nuclear Age*. New York: Random House, 2011.

Seligman, Martin E. P. *Authentic Happiness*. New York: Free Press, 2002.

Sinnott-Armstrong, Walter, and Hanna Pickard. "What Is Addiction?" In *Oxford Handbook of Philosophy and Psychiatry*, edited by K. W. M. Fulford et al., 851–64. Oxford: Oxford University Press, 2013.

Smith, Vernon L. "Constructivist and Ecological Rationality in Economics." *American Economic Review* 93:3 (2003) 465–508.

Snyder, Gary. *The Real Work: Interviews and Talks 1964–1979*. New York: New Directions, 1980.

Steinbeck, John. *The Log from the Sea of Cortez*. New York: Viking, 1951

Steiner, George. *Real Presences*. Chicago: University of Chicago Press, 1989.

Tolle, Eckhart. *The New Earth: Awakening to Your Life's Purpose*. New York: Dutton, 2005.

Sunstein, Cass R. "John and Harriet: Still Mysterious." *New York Review of Books*, April 2, 2015. https://www.nybooks.com/articles/2015/04/02/john-stuart-mill-harriet-taylor-hayek/.

Sutherland, John. "Living on Paper: Letters from Iris Murdoch, 1934–1995." *New York Times Book Review*, January 22, 2016. https://www.nytimes.com/2016/01/24/books/review/living-on-paper-letters-from-iris-murdoch-1934–1995.html

Tatar, Maria. *The Heroine with 1001 Faces*. New York: Penguin, 2021.

Thorp, Charley Linden. "Mahayana Buddhism." *World History Encyclopedia*, 2017. https://www.worldhistory.org/Mahayana_Buddhism/.

Timberman, David G. *Philippine Politics under Duterte: A Mid-Term Assessment*. Washington, DC: Carnegie Endowment for International Peace, January 2019.

https://carnegieendowment.org/2019/01/10/philippine-politics-under-duterte-midterm-assessment-pub-78091.

Valikhani, Ahmad, et al. "The Relationship between Dispositional Gratitude and Quality of Life: The Mediating Role of Perceived Stress and Mental Health." *Personality and Individual Differences* 141 (2019) 40–46.

Visser, Margaret. *The Gift of Thanks.* Boston: Houghton Mifflin Harcourt, 2009.

Waldner, David, and Ellen Lust. "Unwelcome Change: Coming to Terms with Democratic Backsliding." *Annual Review of Political Science* 21:1 (2018) 93–113.

Wardle, H. Newell. "Gifts and Display." In *Encyclopedia of the Social Sciences*, vol. 5/6, edited by David L. Sills. New York: Macmillan, 1968.

The Way of a Pilgrim and The Pilgrim Continues His Way. Translated by Olga Savin. Boston and London: Shambala, 2013.

Weber, Max. "Politics as a Vocation." In *From Max Weber: Essays in Sociology*, edited and translated by H. H. Gerth and C. Wright Mills, 77–128. Oxford: Oxford University Press, 1946. First published 1919.

———. *The Protestant Ethic and the Spirit of Capitalism.* Translated by Peter Baehr and Gordon C. Wells. New York: Penguin, 2002. First published 1905.

———. "Science as a Vocation." In *From Max Weber: Essays in Sociology*, edited and translated by H. H. Gerth and C. Wright Mills, 129–56. Oxford: Oxford University Press, 1946. First published 1919.

Wells, Lisa. *Believers: Making a Life at the End of the World.* New York: Farrar, Straus and Giroux, 2021.

Wilde, Oscar. *The Complete Works of Oscar Wilde.* Vol. 6. New York: National Library, 1909.

Wilder, Thornton. *The Bridge of San Luis Rey.* New York: HarperCollins, 2004. First published 1927.

———. *Heaven's My Destination.* New York: HarperCollins, 2003. First published 1934.

Wilson, Liz. "Ascetic Practices." In *Encyclopedia of Buddhism*, vol. 1, edited by Robert E. Buswell Jr., 280–81. New York: Macmillan Reference, 2004.

———. "Buddhism and Asceticism." In *Oxford Bibliographies in Buddhism*, edited by Richard Payne. New York: Oxford University Press, 2015. https://www.oxfordbibliographies.com/view/document/obo-9780195393521/obo-9780195393521-0206.xml.

Worthington, Everett L., and Scott T. Allison. *Heroic Humility: What the Science of Humility Can Say to People Raised on Self-Focus.* Washington, DC: American Psychological Association, 2018.

Zimbardo, Philip G., et al. "'Exclusive' and 'Inclusive' Visions of Heroism and Democracy." *Current Psychology* 32:3 (2013) 221–33.

———. "What Makes a Hero?" *Greater Good Magazine: Science-Based Insights for a Meaningful Life.* January 18, 2011. https://greatergood.berkeley.edu/article/item/what_makes_a_hero#thank-influence.

Zimmerman, Samuel, and Tomer Ullman. "Models of Transformative Decision-Making." In *Becoming Someone New: Essays on Transformative Experience, Choice, and Change*, edited by Enoch Lambert and John Schwenkler, 73–99. Oxford: Oxford University Press, 2020.

Index